BIBLE STORIES FOR ADULTS

THE STORIES BEHIND THESE FAMILIAR CHILDHOOD TALES.

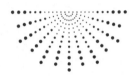

JACK KELLEY

Grace thru Faith

BIBLE STORIES—FOR ADULTS

VOLUMES I & II

OLD & NEW TESTAMENT STORIES

JACK KELLEY

gracethrufaith.com

Grace thru Faith

PO Box 189010-185

Coronado, CA 92178

www.gracethrufaith.com

Bible Stories for Adults / Jack Kelley. —2nd ed.

ISBN 978-1978369962

FOREWORD

My husband Jack was an amazing Bible teacher. He had a gift of making complex topics easy to understand, and communicated God's heart for His people in ways that profoundly influenced his audience.

One of Jack's most popular series has been his *Children's Stories of the Bible for Adults, Volume I.*

Shortly after publishing these Old Testament stories, we were called to be missionaries in Mexico. (You can read the whole story on the Timeline from our About page on gracethrufaith.com.)

From the very beginning, our ministry focused on showing that the God we serve is real, that He hears our prayers and answers them. We asked the Lord only to provide for our needs and the needs of those we served. And He provided abundantly. He is faithful!

From Mexico, Jack published two other books, over 8,000 Bible Q&A posts, and over 1,000 Bible Study articles at gracethrufaith.com. He taught and wrote prolifically, while we provided food, housing, medical care, and education for the poor. Jack was putting the finishing touches on Volume II, the New Testament stories, when he passed away in October 2015.

In the two years since the love of my life went to his eternal home, the Lord continues to prove faithful. Jack's legacy lives on in his teachings on the site, and our outreaches continue to grow. We are able to do more to help those in need now than ever before. As always, we offer all of Jack's teachings free of charge. And we bless those in need with what we're given.

Now, I am so blessed to present to you Jack's teachings on the children's stories in the Bible. In this new book, including Volumes I and II—the Old Testament and New Testament—you'll discover how the language, customs and culture of Biblical times will help you grow in a more mature understanding of these timeless children's stories. I'm excited for you! The details and symbolism of these stories are about to make the Word of God come alive in your heart. Prepare to have your faith strengthened as you grow closer to the Lord.

May the Lord richly bless you,

Samantha Kelley

gracethrufaith.com

INTRODUCTION

The children's stories of the Bible are often a child's first glimpse of God, and the simple way in which they're told is great for little minds. Recent surveys show that most adults who call themselves Christians still believe these stories from their childhoods to be true.

But most of us have never heard the adult versions with their additional detail and background—information that not only enhances their validity but reveals additional insight into the character of God.

And for non-believers who've relegated them to the status of fairy tales and fables, this additional background provides logical and rational reasons to re-think their decision and look at these children's stories again. As you'll see, they're actual events that describe God's earliest revelation of Himself to us.

Here then, are the adult versions of the Bible's children's stories, with detail and background to support the fact that these stories aren't just a Biblical version of Aesop's Fables. They really happened, and for good reason. Over the decades I've been studying them, I've uncovered a wealth of information, which I've pieced together into my view of the story behind each story. I hope reading them will prompt more intense study on your part, to see if these things are true.

For everything that was written in the past was written to teach us, so that through endurance and the encouragement of the Scriptures we might have hope (**Romans 15:4**).

PART I

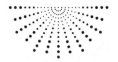

The Old Testament

CHAPTER ONE

CREATION PART 1: IN THE BEGINNING

WHAT HAPPENED BETWEEN GENESIS 1:1 AND 1:2?

> In the beginning God created the heavens and the earth. Now the earth was formless and empty, darkness was over the surface of the deep, and the Spirit of God was hovering over the waters.
>
> And God said, "Let there be light," and there was light. God saw that the light was good, and he separated the light from the darkness. God called the light "day," and the darkness he called "night." And there was evening, and there was morning—the first day.
>
> And God said, "Let there be a vault between the waters to separate water from water." So God made the vault and separated the water under the vault from the water above it. And it was so. God called the vault "sky." And there was evening, and there was morning —the second day. (**Genesis 1:1-8**)

THE STORY BEHIND THE STORY

A quick lesson in Hebrew is helpful to understand verse 1. The Bible uses three Hebrew words to describe creation events:

1. **Bara** literally means *to create* and always refers to a direct work of God. It's the word used in verse 1 and means *to make something from nothing*.

2. **Asah** means *to make something from something else*, and

3. **Yatsar** means *to form or fashion something* as a sculptor or potter might do.

(**Genesis 1:26-27** uses both **bara** and **asah** when speaking of Man's creation, and all three are used together in **Isaiah 45:18** concerning Earth.)

Shamayim, translated *Heavens* in verse one, is what we would call the sky. The word is plural because it includes both the Earth's atmosphere and the vast reaches of space where the stars and other celestial bodies reside. The Bible distinguishes between the atmosphere and the expanse of space, calling them the first and second Heavens respectively. The third Heaven is, of course, the Throne of God.

When the Bible says the *firmament* (or *vault*) separates the waters above from those below, the Hebrew word is **raqiya**. This is Earth's atmosphere—the first Heaven.

Before the Great Flood, this firmament supported a water vapor canopy that enveloped the Earth and deflected harmful ultraviolet rays preventing them from damaging life on Earth, hence the notion of separating waters above from those below.

So the water vapor canopy separated the atmosphere from space— the first Heaven from the second. It also made for a uniformly sunny subtropical climate the world over with no variation in weather patterns. No rain, storms, floods or even heavy winds would have occurred on Earth before the Flood.

Verse 2 is a horse of a different color. Many scholars believe the verse should read, *but the Earth **became** formless and void, an uninhabitable ruin.* Apparently, combining a strict use of grammar with clarifying passages elsewhere in the Old Testament leads to a hint of some sort of judgment between verses 1 and 2 that left the Earth in shambles, an uninhabitable ruin.

The controversy revolves around two issues:

1. Whether the Hebrew requires an active (became) rather than passive (was) form and

2. The Hebrew words **tohu** and **bohu**, translated *formless* and *void.*

These words are found only in **Genesis 1:2, Isaiah 45:18** and **Jeremiah 4:23.** In the Isaiah passage, the Lord reveals that He didn't create the world in vain (the Hebrew is **tohu**) but formed it to be inhabited, thus supporting the idea that it became an uninhabitable ruin. And in a vision, Jeremiah saw Earth when it was formless and void (**tohu** and **bohu**) in the context of a judgment.

THE GAP THEORY

Viewed this way, the first two verses of Genesis would go something like this:

> In the beginning, God created the Heavens and the Earth. As you would expect of God, everything He created was complete, perfect and beautiful, ready for habitation. But then something caused a judgment that left the Earth an uninhabitable ruin for who knows how long. It was dark and wet and cold, but the Spirit of God never left the scene, and after some extended period of time, God said, "Let there be light."

And so, what we know as the Creation account actually begins in verse 3.

This view, known as the Gap Theory, helps solve the so-called "old Earth young civilization" problem. It also reconciles several other issues between creationists and other scientists. By the way, don't try to use the Gap Theory to explain fossils. Death came into the world through sin, and that came after Adam and Eve arrived. Fossils were formed only once in the Earth's history, during the Great Flood.

WHERE DID THEY COME FROM?

What could have caused such a judgment? Some rabbinical scholars contend that the way the first letter was formed in the first Hebrew word of **Genesis 1** warns us that nothing preceding it can be known.

Some hints, though, can lead us to informed speculation. For instance, in **Job 38:7** we see the angels shouting for joy at the **Genesis 1** creation events. Where did the angels come from?

In **Genesis 3** "the shining one" in the form of a serpent tempts Adam and Eve in the Garden. He's described as a created being in **Ezekiel 28:13**, but when was he created? And in **Isaiah 14:12-20** and **Ezekiel 28:11-19** we read of a rebellion and judgment in Heaven.

The King James identifies the one rebelling in Isaiah as Lucifer. From Ezekiel, we learn he was created as an anointed cherub, in charge of the guardians of the Throne of God, and a visitor in the Garden of Eden.

Surely these are references to the rebellion, judgment, and fall of Satan—events that began before the creation of man and will conclude at the end of the Millennium. Could they have also brought about a judgment of the Earth before Adam? Many informed scholars speculate just that.

Speculation? Yes. Will we ever fully understand? Not until we get to Heaven. But I think using the Bible as its own commentary presents compelling, though circumstantial, evidence that favors the Gap Theory. In the next chapter, we'll look at the length of each creation day, discover why the Jews have always begun their day at sunset, and learn when time began.

CHAPTER TWO

CREATION PART TWO: LET THERE BE LIGHT

WHY DO JEWISH DAYS BEGIN AT SUNSET?

> And God said, "Let there be light," and there was light. God saw that the light was good, and he separated the light from the darkness. God called the light "day," and the darkness he called "night." And there was evening, and there was morning—the first day. (**Genesis 1:3-5**)

SHEDDING SOME LIGHT IN THE SUBJECT

I've begun this chapter with **Genesis 1:3-5** because I believe this is where the creation account begins. How could there be light on Day One when the sun and moon didn't appear until Day Four? Like so many things, the answer lies in the Hebrew language.

The word translated **light** in verse 3 is **owr** meaning *illumination.* In verse 14, speaking of the sun and moon, the Hebrew word is

maowr meaning *a luminous body, or light repository*. The word literally means *chandelier*.

In making the sun and moon, God was gathering the light into repositories that would provide it according to schedule.

Note that in referring to the sun and moon, the Hebrew word **asah** (*to make something from something else*) is used rather than **bara** (*to create something from nothing*).

Like a chandelier, the sun and moon are not the light itself but were designed to hold, disperse, or reflect the light.

GOD SPEAKS HEBREW

In calling the light Day, He used the Hebrew word **yom**, a word that appears 2,244 times in Scripture. 1,977 (over 88%) of those appearances clearly refer to *a 24-hour period*. And simple observation of nature tells us the growth cycle of nearly every living thing is based upon alternating periods of darkness and light in relatively short intervals. Life as we know it could not long exist on any other cycle. This makes the view of long Creation "days" (where years and years of light were followed by years and years of darkness) difficult to imagine.

The question is not how could God work so fast, but why did He take so long? Since He could have created it all in the blink of an eye, He was apparently creating a set interval.

The words **darkness** and **night** are also direct translations of **chosek** and **laylah** respectively. The only reason to interpret these words figuratively instead of literally, is if you're trying to reconcile evolution with creation—an impossible task.

On the other hand, the words for **evening** and **morning** provide a wealth of information when viewed in the original.

Their roots also reveal the reason God began the day at sunset rather than midnight. Dr. Gerald L. Schroeder is a Hebrew scholar with a doctorate in physics from MIT. I had the good fortune to meet him in Jerusalem on one of my trips to Israel.

In his book, *Genesis and the Big Bang*, Dr. Schroeder explains that according to ancient Hebrew sages, the word for **evening**, **erev**, comes from a root meaning *mixed up, stirred together, disorderly*.

It brings to mind the confusion we sometimes experience just at dusk when the mixed-up light and darkness can cause our eyes to play tricks on us. **Boker**, the word for **morning**, comes from a root meaning *discernible, able to be distinguished, or orderly*. This word recalls the returning clarity of vision that accompanies dawn.

FROM DISORDER TO ORDER

As a physicist familiar with the Second Law of Thermodynamics (the Law of Entropy), Dr. Schroeder was astonished.

Simply stated, the Law of Entropy explains that when left alone everything in the universe will deteriorate from order into disorder. For simple examples, just look around you. Even when you apply a regular program of maintenance to slow the process, everything you own, your home, your car, even your body will eventually fall apart and stop working. Entropy is a natural law—like Newton's Laws of Motion and Gravity—and cannot be reversed.

By using these words for **evening** and **morning** in their particular order, God reveals that in each day of creation He was overruling the Law of Entropy. He was bringing disorder into order.

This demolishes any argument that the Earth came to be by accident or coincidence, or that man could have evolved from animals that evolved from fish, etc. Such a natural phenomenon is in and of itself impossible since it requires that nature violates a fundamental natural law.

Only an external creative power superior to natural law could have brought about Earth and its inhabitants.

To make sure we get the point, God repeated the phrase six times, one for each day of creation, and caused His people to begin their day at sunset. Every day since then the Hebrew calendar has reminded man of God's superiority over the laws of nature, by saying, "First there was evening (disorder) then there was morning (order)."

IT'S ABOUT TIME

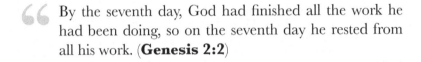

> By the seventh day, God had finished all the work he had been doing, so on the seventh day he rested from all his work. (**Genesis 2:2**)

According to some Rabbinical sources, the underlying meaning of this verse explains no less than the beginning of time.

God completed the work of creation and placed man on Earth to subdue and take dominion over it. God then rested, setting in motion all the laws that would govern man's existence, including the duration of the day, the week, the month and the year.

These time references were all established during the six days of creation and would remain throughout man's tenure on Earth.

Now you know the adult version.

CHAPTER THREE

ADAM AND EVE

NEW INSIGHTS INTO THE OLDEST STORY IN HISTORY

There was such peace and harmony in the Garden. Every need was met, every desire of the heart fulfilled. Scholars speculate on the length of time Adam and Eve enjoyed in the Eden, but no one really knows. I believe it was long enough to give them a very clear perspective on the differences they would experience after the fall. Life in the Garden is so deeply imprinted in the memory of man that it's been the stuff of mythology and the subject of books ever since. Sir Thomas More's book *Utopia* is perhaps the most famous example.

WHOSE STORY IS THIS?

Some scholars point to differences between Genesis chapters 1 and 2 that hint of inconsistency in the creation account, but there's a simple explanation. The Book of Genesis consists of 10 sections, each the account of a different patriarch. But all brought together by a single author, the Holy Spirit, working through the hand of Moses. Each section begins with the phrase "these are the generations" (KJV) or "this is the account" (NIV). Only God was around for chapter 1, but beginning with chapter 2, Genesis describes events from the perspective of Adam and his descendants. Some even assert that Moses had possession of written accounts from Adam, and others, and drew upon them in compiling the book. Since archaeologists have discovered great libraries from pre-flood times, this view has merit.

THE SERPENT IN THE GARDEN

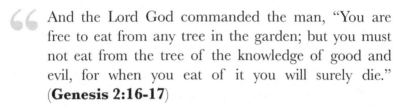 And the Lord God commanded the man, "You are free to eat from any tree in the garden; but you must not eat from the tree of the knowledge of good and evil, for when you eat of it you will surely die." (**Genesis 2:16-17**)

Now the serpent was more crafty than any of the wild animals the Lord God had made. He said to the woman, "Did God really say, 'You must not eat from any tree in the garden?'" (**Genesis 3:1**)

The startlingly obvious fact that Eve was okay conversing with a serpent tells us more was going on than we realize. The word translated **serpent** literally means *enchanter,* so what we know about a serpent's appearance was learned after its judgment. I can't imagine any man or woman being comfortable talking with a snake today.

DID GOD REALLY SAY ...

Most people assume Satan had indwelt the serpent and was manipulating it, but the way God pronounced a curse upon it tells us the serpent was not just an innocent victim of circumstances, but was a culpable participant. It's also interesting that the prophecy of Satan's ultimate defeat by the seed of the woman (a Messianic reference) was contained within the curse God pronounced upon the serpent (**Genesis 3:15**).

The serpent's first question formed the basis for all man's disobedience ever since. It sounds so reasonable, but think of all the undermining of His Word that begins with that phrase.

Did God really say that life begins at conception? (**Ecclesiastes 11:5**) Did He really say there's no other God but Him? (**Isaiah 46:8-9**) Did God really say we're saved by grace alone? (**Ephesians 2:8-9**) Or that we must be born again? (**John 3:3**) The list goes on. Get the idea?

LIFE IN THE GARDEN

> When the woman saw that the fruit of the tree was good for food and pleasing to the eye, and also desirable for gaining wisdom, she took some and ate it. She also gave some to her husband, who was with her, and he ate it. (**Genesis 3:6**)

There were all kinds of trees in the garden that were pleasing to the eye and good for eating, but **Genesis 2:9** makes specific reference to two of them, the tree of life and the tree of the knowledge of good and evil. Before Eve was created, God warned Adam against eating the fruit of the tree of the knowledge of good and evil (**Genesis 2:16-17**). Since Eve explained this rule to the serpent (**Genesis 3:2**) she had been told as well.

Somehow, the fruit of the tree of life sustained their immortality, while eating fruit from the tree of the knowledge of good and evil made them mortal, subject to death, and that's why it was forbidden. We were not created to be merely mortal, but to dwell in the house of the Lord forever.

WHO TOLD YOU THAT YOU WERE NAKED?

When they ate from the forbidden tree, the eyes of both were opened and they realized they were naked, so they sewed fig leaves together and made coverings for themselves (**Genesis 3:7**). Here is the first act of religion: our vain attempt to cover ourselves before a Holy God. But God showed them a better way. The Lord made garments of animal skin for Adam and Eve and clothed them (**Genesis 3:21**). It was by the shedding of innocent animal blood that they would be covered. This event initiated the sacrificial system for setting aside man's sin, a Messianic model. For Christ died for sins once for all, the righteous for the unrighteous to bring you to God (**1 Peter 3:18**). Note that sacrificing an innocent animal could only set aside man's sin. It took the shed blood of an innocent man to truly redeem mankind. More on that later.

In the Interlinear Bible, a direct Hebrew to English translation, the root of the word translated **naked** in **Genesis 2:25** literally means *to be empty or poured out,* or figuratively, *naive or child-like.* In **Genesis 3:10** a different word is translated naked. It comes from a root meaning *crafty* or *cunning,* and is used in **Genesis 3:1** to describe the serpent. Interesting. In their desire to become like God as the serpent had promised, Adam and Eve actually became like the serpent. They now knew both good and evil, but could not control the evil.

WHOSE DECISION WAS IT?

What took Adam and Eve out of the Garden? Nothing more than the substitution of their own will for God's. He had given them everything, including the freedom from worry. He had accepted full responsibility for their well-being, providing for them physically, mentally, emotionally, and spiritually.

When they began making decisions for themselves, He let them. But He also let them share some of the responsibility for their decisions. This shared responsibility brought them feelings unknown in the creation until then. The Hebrew word describing these feelings is translated *sorrow* in the KJV and *pain* or *painful toil* in the NIV. It's used only three times. Two of those are in **Genesis 3:16-17**, verses that outline the consequences of their decisions.

The point to remember is this. Adam and Eve learned that sorrow and painful toil came into their lives as the result of seeking independence from God.

SHARED RESPONSIBILITY

When I say the Lord let them share some of the responsibility, here's what I mean. They had just made what would be the second biggest mistake in the history of Man (the biggest would be Israel's murder of their Messiah). And God could have made them disappear and started again with another handful of red dirt **(Genesis 2:7)**. But instead, He loved them, watched over them, and cared for them as His children.

His first act of kindness after the fall was to provide food for them, even though they had to work for it. His second was to clothe them. His third was to send Cherubim to guard the way to the Tree of Life, preserving their way back to the Garden once the consequences of their actions had been reversed at the cross **(Romans 8:20-21)**.

In no way could Adam and Eve negate the outcome of their decision. But because of His great mercy, they could learn from it and voluntarily yield their will back to the Lord who was still their Provider (El Shaddai). When they did, He blessed them with long lives and many children—signs of His favor. And though their circumstances were forever changed, they again walked and talked with God and were at peace with Him in spite of those circumstances. In other words, even though they could no longer physically live in the Garden, they could achieve a Garden state of mind.

LESSONS FROM HISTORY

The German philosopher Hegel once said, "The only thing we learn from history is that we learn nothing from history." But in **Romans 15:4** Paul wrote, "Everything that was written in the past was written to teach us, so that through endurance and the encouragement of the Scriptures, we might have hope."

In other words, lessons that began in the Garden still apply today. We're to learn both from Adam and Eve's mistakes and the Lord's response.

Like Adam and Eve, we're God's people, His kids. He desires to have a relationship with us. He wants to bless us and protect us inside that relationship. As long as we abide in Him and align ourselves with His will, our every need will be met and He will assume full responsibility for our well-being (**Psalm 37:4 & Matthew 6:31-33**). But when we don't, He begins sharing the responsibility with us. The more we act apart from Him, the more responsibility He shares. Along with shared responsibility come sorrow and painful toil.

When we align our will with His again, He takes the responsibility back. Since He hasn't given us full use of the dimension of time, we can't go back and negate the consequences of our independent decisions. But like Adam and Eve, we can learn from them and abide in Him again. All He requires is confession and a willingness to start over. His mercies are new every morning, so we too can achieve a Garden state of mind in spite of our circumstances, just like our first parents.

IT'S ALL IN YOUR MIND

One day soon, the Lord will lead us all back to the real Garden, the one in Heaven. But until then, there's the Garden state of mind. These are perilous times. If you're stressed out about them, maybe you're assuming too much responsibility, trying to impose your own will on things you can't control instead of trusting God and living according to His will. If so, you're living outside the Garden, where it's full of sorrow and painful toil.

Jesus said, "Come to Me all you who are weary and heavy-laden, and I will give you rest." (**Matthew 11:28**)

Give your life to Him again, and relieve yourself of the responsibility. You may not be able to reverse the effects of your past decisions, but if you draw near to Him, He'll draw near to you and lead you safely through them. Just like Adam and Eve did, you'll find that life's better in the Garden, even when it's only a state of mind.

Now you know the adult version.

CHAPTER FOUR

CAIN AND ABEL

WHY DIDN'T GOD LIKE CAIN'S OFFERING?

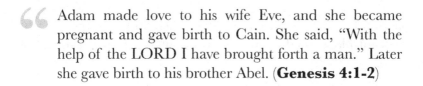

> Adam made love to his wife Eve, and she became pregnant and gave birth to Cain. She said, "With the help of the LORD I have brought forth a man." Later she gave birth to his brother Abel. (**Genesis 4:1-2**)

The Hebrew root for **Cain** means *to procure*, while **Abel** means *transitory* or *meaningless*. From Eve's comment and Cain's name, we discover that the Lord had delegated the procreation process. This enables obedience to His command to multiply and fill the Earth (**Genesis 1:28**) without requiring a direct act of creation for each person born. We can also assume from Abel's name that Eve believed Cain would be her Redeemer and therefore felt Abel was unnecessary.

Discovering the meanings of Biblical names can be so fascinating. Whether it's a person or place, you'll almost always gain added insight into the passage.

> Now Abel kept flocks and Cain worked the soil. In the course of time Cain brought some of the fruits of the soil as an offering to the LORD. And Abel also brought an offering—fat portions from some of the firstborn of his flock. The LORD looked with favor on Abel and his offering, but on Cain and his offering he did not look with favor. So Cain was very angry and his face was downcast. Then the LORD said to Cain, "Why are you so angry? Why is your face downcast? If you do what is right will you not be accepted? But if you do not do what is right, sin is crouching at your door; it desires to have you, but you must master it." **(Genesis 4:2-7)**

EVERYTHING WRITTEN IN THE PAST WAS WRITTEN TO TEACH US

Here we learn that the remedy for sin was first taught to Adam in the Garden, not to Moses at Mt. Sinai.

By offering the firstborn from his flock, Abel illustrated the concept of innocent blood shed for the remission of sin, again, a model of the Messiah.

Cain brought the works of his own hands, an offering of thanksgiving. Because the Lord reminded Cain to "do what is right" it's clear He had instructed them on this.

The sin offering, an act of confession, purifies us and permits us reentry into the presence of God. Only then will our offerings of praise and thanksgiving be acceptable. Formalized in the Levitical system, and simplified in **1 John 1:8-10**, this was actually revealed at the instant of the first sin. It demonstrates our need for a Redeemer while teaching the futility of either providing our own remedy for our sins or ignoring them altogether (as Cain did) both of which are offensive to God.

CONFESS EARLY AND OFTEN

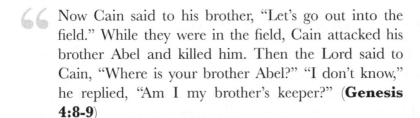

> Now Cain said to his brother, "Let's go out into the field." While they were in the field, Cain attacked his brother Abel and killed him. Then the Lord said to Cain, "Where is your brother Abel?" "I don't know," he replied, "Am I my brother's keeper?" (**Genesis 4:8-9**)

As was the case with his father Adam, the Lord asked Cain the question, not because He was seeking information, but because He was seeking confession.

Adam gave a flimsy excuse (it was the woman's fault) but Cain showed callous indifference. In fact, isn't it hard to see anything good in Cain's behavior? He ignored the Lord's command about offerings and then became angry when his offering was rejected. Instead of confessing, he let his anger become jealousy toward Abel and lured him into the field for a premeditated act of murder. Then he lied about it and expressed only indifference when confronted. Little sins, left unchecked, become big ones (**James 1:15**).

The Lord's warning, "Sin is crouching at your door and desires to have you," bears a closer look. The Hebrew word translated **crouching** was used in ancient times to describe the way a demon would lie in wait for a victim. Perhaps because of this passage, the word **desire** is the same one used to describe Eve's attitude toward Adam in **Genesis 3:16,** meaning *to long for*. Our enemy has a passionate interest in us and will lie in wait, longing for the opportunities presented by our sins. Having failed to apply the prescribed remedy for sin, Cain was fair game and the enemy took full advantage. Please remember, Cain had a relationship with God. He spoke with God and was taught directly by Him, and still committed a grievous sin. It's a striking example of the pervasiveness of the sin nature introduced into the human gene pool at the fall and should remind us of our tendency toward sin, no matter how "spiritual" we think we are, or how firmly rooted in our faith. (See **1 Peter 5:8 & 1 John 1:8-10.**)

THE MARK OF CAIN: A MODEL OF GRACE

So Cain was driven from the land to live as a fugitive and vagabond. He was afraid he would be forever banished from the presence of God and deprived of His protection. "Not so," said the Lord, and put His mark on Cain saving his life (**Genesis 4:15**). The collective mind of scholarship has been probed in vain to determine the nature of this mark, but that's not the point. All through the chapter, the covenant name of God has been used, indicating the scope of Cain's relationship with Him. Cain sinned and refused to confess, and therefore put himself out of fellowship with God. But God didn't revoke His covenant, nor did He withdraw His protection.

Unconfessed sin interrupts our relationship with God and causes us to wander in spiritual wilderness, but it doesn't sever our family ties and it doesn't put our eternal life at risk.

Cain serves as a model of so many Christians today.

When we, as believers, refuse to recognize and confess our sins, we are out of fellowship with God. But we are still in His family and still have eternal (protected) lives. While out of fellowship, we are objects of the enemy's passionate interest, and fair game for his schemes against us, but our union with God and eternal destiny are marked by His Grace as off limits to the stealer of men's souls. For more on this, listen to my audio Bible study on Union and Fellowship.

Jesus was our sacrifice. All we need to do now is confess. And immediately, we are forgiven. The slate is wiped clean, the Lord chooses to forget we ever sinned in the first place, and we are back in fellowship with Him.

Now you know the adult version.

CHAPTER FIVE

NOAH AND THE FLOOD PART ONE

WHAT ARE THE FOUR SCARIEST VERSES IN THE BIBLE?

> When human beings began to increase in number on the earth and daughters were born to them, the sons of God saw that the daughters of humans were beautiful, and they married any of them they chose. Then the Lord said, "My Spirit will not contend with humans forever, for they are mortal; their days will be a hundred and twenty years." The Nephilim were on the earth in those days—and also afterward—when the sons of God went to the daughters of humans and had children by them. They were the heroes of old, men of renown. (**Genesis 6:1-4**)

Take this literally, as we always do, and it's four of the scariest verses in the Bible. The Hebrew phrase translated *sons of God* refers to beings who are direct creations of God, typically angels, and it distinguishes the origin of the males in the passage from that of the females.

Only two human males are ever described this way, Adam (**Luke 3:38**) and the Lord Jesus. In **Psalm 82:6** the rulers of Israel are called children of the Most High, but the context refers to their role as judges of the people, responsible for dispensing both justice and mercy. In **John 1:12**, we who have received the Lord into our hearts are given the authority to become children of God. But there the notion is that of being born again as a *spiritual* child of God, a concept amplified in **John 3:3-21**.

THE TESTIMONY OF TWO WITNESSES

To make sure we get the point of **Genesis 6:1-4**, the distinction appears twice. The males were direct creations of God while the females were the offspring of human parents. The passage clearly implies that fallen angels somehow took on the form of human males and married human females who bore their children. **2 Peter 2:4** and **Jude 6** mention these fallen angels as having been rounded up and bound in chains awaiting the Judgment Day, and in **1 Corinthians 6:3** Paul hinted that the Church will judge them for their actions. Their children were called Nephilim, a Hebrew word that translates *fallen ones* and were destroyed in the Flood (The Greek word is **gigantes**—the origin of our word *giant*).

But Nephilim also appeared after the Flood as foretold in **Genesis 6:4** (where it says they "were on the earth in those days—and also afterward"). Returning from their first view of the Promised Land, the 12 spies reported seeing them among the local population (**Numbers 13:33**). This is one reason the Lord instructed the Israelites to wipe out all the people of Canaan (**Deuteronomy 20:16-18**) including their animals before settling down in their new land. Like Nephilim, the Rephaim were also called giants and are mentioned throughout the Old Testament. Goliath was from the Rephaim.

Mythological figures like Hercules and other demigods are actually representations of the Nephilim, woven into the pagan religions of ancient times. In this way, the fallen angels received the worship they coveted.

BACK TO GENESIS

The mixed marriages of **Genesis 6** contaminated the human gene pool. Satan was trying to thwart the plan of God by preventing the birth of a Redeemer, since a direct descendant of Adam was required, a man without sin. Man sinned, allowing Evil into the world, and God had to destroy His contaminated creation and begin again. It's a dreadful thing to fall into the hands of the Living God (**Hebrews 10:31**).

BUT NOAH FOUND GRACE IN THE EYES OF THE LORD

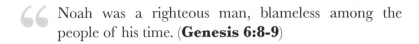 Noah was a righteous man, blameless among the people of his time. (**Genesis 6:8-9**)

The Hebrew here means *perfect in his generations*—not sinless. Within the above context, it's clear God chose Noah for two reasons. First, his genealogy was not contaminated by intermarriage so a direct line to Adam could be preserved, and second, Noah was faithful. Even in the worst of times the Lord has always preserved a faithful remnant to begin again. And Noah, though a sinner like all men, had walked with God all his life.

Genesis 6:5-6 says that every intention of man's mind was evil and God saw no alternative to destroying them all. He had given mankind 10 generations, great teachers like Enoch, a living reminder in Methuselah (the name means *his death shall bring*) and a 120-year countdown (**Genesis 6:3**). In the year Methuselah died the Great Flood came, 1,656 years after Adam's creation. And the record shows not one of the world's inhabitants joined Noah on the

Ark. Just like the people of our time, they didn't believe God would ever judge them. Like Hegel said, "The only thing we learn from history is that we never learn anything from history."

Now you know the adult version.

CHAPTER SIX

NOAH AND THE FLOOD PART TWO: THE BIG BOAT

WAS THE ARK BIG ENOUGH TO DO THE JOB?

> God saw how corrupt the earth had become, for all the people on earth had corrupted their ways. So God said to Noah, "I am going to put an end to all people for the earth is filled with violence because of them. I am surely going to destroy both them and the earth. So make yourself an ark out of cypress wood, make rooms in it and coat it with pitch inside and out. This is how you are to build it: the ark is to be 450 feet long, 75 feet wide and 45 feet high. Make a roof for the ark and finish it to within 18 inches of the top. Put a door in the side of the ark and make lower, middle, and upper decks. (**Genesis 6:12-16**)

Let's address three of the arguments scoffers use, trying to discredit the notion of a worldwide flood through which a human family, together with pairs of every animal variety, were preserved in a big boat.

THAT'S A BIG BOAT

But was the Ark big enough? 450 feet is one and a half times the length of a football field. Stood on end, the Ark would be about as tall as a 45-story office building. At 75 feet wide, each of the Ark's three decks contained 33,750 square feet of floor space, for a total of 101,250. Since the Ark was 4.5 stories tall (45 feet), there was over 1.5 million cubic feet of space under its roof, equivalent to a train with 500 boxcars. If you take every animal, from a mouse to an elephant, and average their size, you'll find that sheep are exactly average. I'm told that shippers allocate about 250 sheep per boxcar when moving them by train. A train with 500 cars would accommodate 125,000 sheep or 62,500 pairs.

Zoologists recognize about 18,000 species of animals today, so if Noah went by the same figures, he would have needed room for about 18,000 pairs of animals or 36,000 total plus five more of every "clean" variety and every bird species (**Genesis 7:3**). If the total animal count was about 50,000, it would have taken 40% of the Ark's capacity to house them. Even if they used half of the Ark's total space for food storage, Noah would have had 10,125 square feet left for himself and his family.

I believe the animals were put into some form of hibernation or suspended animation and would have needed very little food. Otherwise, the job of feeding them and cleaning up after them would have been too much for the eight humans on board to handle. Also, there's no mention of either a birth or death among the animal population during the entire 53 weeks they were on board together.

By the way, ever wonder how Noah knew which animals were *clean?* The same way Cain and Abel knew what to bring as an offering. God told them. The Levitical system began in the Garden not in the wilderness. Moses simply put into writing what God's people had always known.

THAT'S A LOT OF WATER

"I am going to bring floodwaters on the Earth to destroy all life under the Heavens, every creature that has the breath of life in it. Everything on Earth will perish (**Genesis 6:17**). Two of every kind of animal and every kind of creature that moves along the ground will come to you" (**Genesis 6:20**). I love the cartoons of Noah running around with butterfly nets trying to catch the animals, when in fact, God the Creator of all living things put it into their heads to come to Noah.

> In the six hundredth year of Noah's life on the seventh day of the second month—on that day all the springs of the great deep burst forth, and the floodgates of heaven were opened. And rain fell on the Earth 40 days and 40 nights. (**Genesis 7:11-12**)

By this, we know that there were enormous supplies of water available for the Flood. First, the springs of the great deep—that up till then had irrigated the Earth (**Genesis 2:5-6**)—were opened up. And then the floodgates of Heaven—a water vapor barrier that had protected the Earth from harmful ultraviolet rays enabling long life spans (**Genesis 1:7-8**)—collapsed. This caused rain—which had never fallen on Earth (**Genesis 2:5-6** and **Hebrews 11:7**) to fall for 40 days and 40 nights.

BUT LORD, YOU PROMISED

> The waters rose and covered the mountains to a depth of more than 20 feet. Everything that moved on the earth perished—birds, livestock, wild animals, all the creatures that swarm on the earth, and all mankind. Everything on dry land that had the breath of life in its nostrils died. (**Genesis 7:20-22**)

Along with the inclusive intent of this passage, two factors argue undeniably for a worldwide flood: the nature of water and the rainbow. Some of the highest mountains on Earth are found in the region, and water seeks its own level. If it covered the mountains there, it would have to cover them everywhere else in the world as well. There are no natural barriers high enough to contain it. And in **Genesis 9:11-17** the Lord promised never to destroy the world by flooding again and put a rainbow in the sky as a token of this promise. There have been many local and regional floods since Noah's time. If Noah's flood was only local, then God has broken His promise over and over again. Arguments against a universal flood are really attempts to deny God's capacity for judgment (**2 Peter 3:3-7**).

Now you know the adult version.

CHAPTER SEVEN

NOAH AND THE FLOOD PART THREE: HIDDEN IN PLAIN SIGHT

WHERE IS NOAH'S ARK TODAY?

Let's go through the account of Noah and the Flood one more time. This time, we'll pick up some of the tidbits that make these stories so exciting—things the Lord often hides in plain sight.

PERFECT PITCH

The Ark was coated with pitch both inside and out (**Genesis 6:14**) which is unusual. The coating on the outside is done to keep a boat waterproof, but the coating on the inside is done to preserve it and ensure a long useful life. Noah only needed the Ark once and only for a year. Did God want it kept for some later use? And then there's the Hebrew word for **pitch**. It comes from a root meaning *atonement, forgiveness,* or *pardon* and is translated pitch only here. What's the hidden clue in this word? Is this a model of God's grace, by which man is pardoned through faith, rescuing him from judgment? Was the Ark a type of Christ—a vessel of salvation? (See **1 Thessalonians 1:9-10**.)

And what about its resting place? You and I would have the Ark land where it could be used as a dwelling or its materials at least cannibalized for other use. Remember, it was as big as a small hotel. Why did the Lord have it land high in the mountains, make Noah leave it, and then hide it? I've heard Bible archaeologists complain that no matter what they discover to support the validity of Biblical accounts, people respond, "That's great. Now if you could just find Noah's Ark." Was the Ark being kept, not for Noah, but for us "upon whom the fulfillment of the ages has come" (**1 Corinthians 10:11**) as the final and irrefutable proof of His existence before the next and final judgment?

BIBLE ARCHAEOLOGY SEARCH AND EXPLORATION INSTITUTE

Bob Cornuke, founder of BASE Institute, claims that Mt. Sinai is not in Egypt, as tradition holds, but in Saudi Arabia. He has been there and stood on the place called The Mountain of Moses in Arabic. Biblical references support his discoveries there, and in talking with him, I'm convinced he's found the real Mount Sinai as well as the route the Israelites took to reach it and the place where they crossed the Red Sea. Bob has also climbed Mount Ararat in Turkey in search of Noah's Ark and wonders if the traditional site for the Ark's location might also be wrong. A literal rendering of **Genesis 11:2** places the mountains of Ararat, mentioned as the Ark's resting place in **Genesis 8:4**, somewhere east of ancient Babylon. Other historical sources agree, and on a map, it looks obvious. Mount Ararat, so named in modern times, is a volcano several hundred miles north. Perhaps, as Bob and others believe, the Ark is really amidst the Zagros Mountains in Iran, not atop a volcano in Turkey. Hidden in plain sight? Go to www.baseinstitute.org for a copy of his book on the subject.

WHAT DAY IS THIS?

And finally, there's the date the Ark came to rest. The 17th day of the 7th month is recognized in Jewish life to this day and is even more prominent in Christianity. Here's why. In **Exodus 12:1** the Lord commanded the Israelites to change their calendar. What had been the 7th month ever since the creation was now to become the first. We know this because they retained the original calendar and superimposed the new one over it. On the religious calendar (the new one) Passover, which falls in spring, is always the 14th day of the first month as commanded in **Exodus 12,** and on the civil calendar (the old one) New Year's Day comes in the fall six months later. So with this six-month offset, what in Noah's day had been the seventh month became the first month of the new religious calendar.

On the 17th day of that month the Ark ran aground, and for the first time, Noah and his family knew from experience that their new life had begun. According to Sir Robert Anderson and the London Royal Observatory, a study of the lunar cycle through the centuries shows it was a Sunday.

Jews celebrate the Feast of First Fruits on the Sunday that follows Passover (**Leviticus 23:9-11**). So each time Passover (the 14th) falls on a Thursday, the Feast of First Fruits is the 17th three days later. Noah and his family were the first fruits of the New World—a world born again.

Two thousand years later on that same date, also a Sunday and the Feast of First Fruits, a sealed tomb in Jerusalem was found open and empty. The Lord had been raised from the dead, the First Fruits of those who have fallen asleep (**1 Corinthians 15:20**). For followers of Jesus, the 17th day of the first month was Resurrection Morning, and for the first time, the disciples knew from experience that their new life had begun. That evening they received the Holy Spirit—men born again (**John 20:19-22**).

Just as the Ark had preserved faithful Noah's family through the prior judgment and became a model of God's Grace, The Lord

Jesus will preserve faithful Israel through the coming judgment, the Personification of Grace. Just as Noah was cast adrift in a world under judgment and experienced the grounding that signified a world born again, a seeker cast adrift in a life under judgment today looks to the cross and the empty tomb and experiences the "grounding" that signifies a life born again.

Now you know the adult version.

CHAPTER EIGHT

THE TOWER OF BABEL

WHAT DEADLY SIN ORIGINATED THERE?

> Now the whole world had one language and a common speech. As people moved eastward, they found a plain in Shinar and settled there. (**Genesis 11:1-2**)

The story of the Tower of Babel begins in **Genesis 11**, but gives us the reason for the formation of the 70 nation (or ethnic) groupings, outlined in **Genesis 10.** The Lord had told Noah and his family to "be fruitful and increase in number and fill the Earth" (**Genesis 9:1**). But Noah's descendants had decided to remain on the plains of Shinar and build a civilization for themselves there, following the pattern of the Cainites (not to be confused with the Canaanites) before the Flood. They determined to "build ourselves a city with a tower that reaches to the Heavens so that we may make a name for ourselves and not be scattered over the face of the Earth" (**Genesis 11:4**). This was contrary to God's instructions, and guaranteed to cause problems.

WHERE ARE WE?

Here's something I find interesting. They settled on the plains of Shinar, an area we know as Mesopotamia, modern Iraq. They had come from the East, or Iran, where the Ark had settled. Beneath this area today lies some of the world's largest known oil reserves. Oil comes from the decomposition of vegetation. And the Tigris and Euphrates rivers that border the area (**Mesopotamia** means *between two rivers*) are mentioned in the Creation account as flowing through the Garden of Eden. When it came to building materials for their city and tower, the people chose tar as a substitute for mortar, since there was no cement handy. Put all this circumstantial evidence together, and you can surmise that the Garden of Eden encompassed the whole region, and was buried under tons and tons of sand after the Flood. The weight of the sand compressed the decaying vegetation and helped produce the oil that then bubbled up out of the ground as tar. But that's a story for another day.

BACK TO BABEL

But the Lord came down to see the city and the tower the men were building (**Genesis 11:6**). Enough of the ruins of the Tower of Babel have been discovered to permit archaeologists to speculate on its appearance and purpose. It covered four acres at its base and was 153 feet tall. There were seven stages, each one smaller than the one below, giving it the appearance of a giant wedding cake. Each stage was dedicated to one of the then known planets, and a tower at the top had the 12 signs of the zodiac inscribed on the walls. It was apparently intended as a combination observatory and temple to enable the people to worship the celestial bodies and practice astrology.

WHAT SIGN ARE YOU?

The 12 signs of the zodiac are a perversion of the Hebrew Mazzaroth. By tradition Adam, Seth, and Enoch named 12 constellations of the stars to foretell the Gospel story. As shepherds lay under the stars at night, fathers could use them to instruct their sons on the Lord's plan of redemption for His fallen people (Read *The Gospel in the Stars* by Joseph A. Seiss). Horoscopes use the Babylonian names of these constellations. These corrupt names are virtually the same in every known language except Hebrew, where the true names and meanings of the 12 signs can be learned. This is why the study of astrology ("observer of times" in the KJV) was an offense punishable by death in Israel and was given as one of the causes for the Canaanites' expulsion from the Promised Land (**Deuteronomy 18:9-11**).

JUSTICE AND MERCY

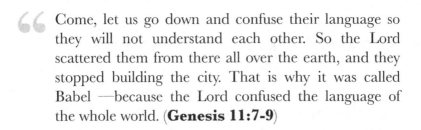

Come, let us go down and confuse their language so they will not understand each other. So the Lord scattered them from there all over the earth, and they stopped building the city. That is why it was called Babel —because the Lord confused the language of the whole world. (**Genesis 11:7-9**)

Once again, an act of judgment contained an element of mercy. By stopping things when He did, the Lord prevented the people from going entirely astray and bringing about their complete destruction. Confusing their language curtailed their misplaced spirit of cooperation, and so they separated, accomplished God's purpose, and escaped a much greater penalty. Hidden in every human effort to unite in a common cause you'll find Satan working to separate us from our Creator. God's will must be our main goal and focus. When it isn't, Satan only needs to appeal to our sense of pride and self-determination to orchestrate our defeat. This is true whether it's a group of individuals or a community of nations.

Now you know the adult version.

CHAPTER NINE

ABRAHAM AND ISAAC: THE GOSPEL IN GENESIS

DID GOD REALLY ASK ABRAHAM TO VIOLATE HIS LAW?

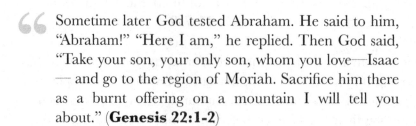

> Sometime later God tested Abraham. He said to him, "Abraham!" "Here I am," he replied. Then God said, "Take your son, your only son, whom you love—Isaac—and go to the region of Moriah. Sacrifice him there as a burnt offering on a mountain I will tell you about." (**Genesis 22:1-2**)

This is perhaps the most misunderstood of all the children's stories. But the clues that will lead us to a correct understanding are hidden in plain sight right in the passage. Some interpretations of this story explain that our Almighty God is so insecure He will force us to make agonizing choices just to prove we really love Him. Is that the case? Or was there more going on than meets the eye? Let's find out.

The first clue is in God's use of Abraham's covenant name. This tells us He had already agreed to bless and protect Abraham and make him the father of many nations. The covenant was unilateral and required no commitment from Abraham to remain in force. (He had put Abraham to sleep during the ceremony.) Also, by calling Isaac Abraham's only son, it's clear God didn't think Isaac was expendable—He intended Isaac as the child of the promise. Surely Ishmael, Abraham's first born would also be blessed, but it was through Isaac that the covenant would be actualized (**Genesis 17:19-22**). Already an interesting parallel is emerging between what God was asking Abraham to do and what He would later do Himself.

YOUR ONLY BELOVED SON

In **John 3:16** Jesus is called God's only son, but is He? **Luke 3:37-38** refers to Adam as the son of God. Adam preceded Jesus in birth order, but Jesus occupies the ceremonial position of firstborn, inheriting all its rights and privileges. He is always referred to as the only Son of God. Ishmael was born to Abraham and Hagar 19 years before Sarah gave birth to Isaac, and according to human law was the legitimate firstborn. But God didn't recognize him as such. Isaac is called Abraham's only son.

And then there's the location—the region of Moriah. Mount Moriah is the place where Solomon would later build the temple (**2 Chronicles 3:1**). Just north of the Temple area, Jesus would be sacrificed as an offering for the sins of the world, on the same spot where Abraham was being asked to offer Isaac.

THREE DAYS AND THREE NIGHTS

 On the third day, Abraham looked up and saw the place in the distance. He said to his servants, "Stay here with the donkey while I and the boy go over there. We will worship and then we will come back to you." Abraham took the wood for the burnt offering

and placed it on his son Isaac, and he himself carried
the fire and the knife. (**Genesis 22:4-6**)

Did God really intend for Abraham to bind Isaac, slit his throat,
place him upon the altar and burn him there? In **Deuteronomy
18:9-13** God expressly forbade such an act. Would He ask
Abraham to do something against His own law? As the two of them
went on together, Isaac spoke up and said to his father Abraham,
"Father?" "Yes my son," Abraham replied. "The fire and the wood
are here but where is the lamb for the burnt offering?" Abraham
answered, "God himself will provide the lamb for the burnt offering, my son." And the two of them went on together (**Genesis
22:6-8**).

GRACE THROUGH FAITH

Hebrews 11:17-19 explains that Abraham did this by faith,
knowing all along that God, who cannot lie, had promised him a
long line of descendants through Isaac, and yet at this time Isaac
had no children. He *reasoned* that God could raise the dead—and
figuratively speaking—he did receive Isaac back from the dead. This
was not just an act of blind faith. Being in a covenant relationship
with God and knowing His nature and character, Abraham trusted
God and placed the outcome in His hands. I believe that along the
way God revealed the details to Abraham, enabling him to tell the
servants that "we will worship and then we will come back to you."
And to tell Isaac that "God himself will provide the lamb for the
burnt offering." The Lord subsequently did this, (**Genesis 22:13**)
and the innocent ram God provided died in Isaac's place.

It fascinates me that this entire drama unfolded over three days and
three nights. By the way, the word that's translated **boy** in verse 6
means *a young man of military age* (18-30). And in verse 8 the word for
together means *united* and comes from a root meaning *to become as
one*. Apparently, Isaac was an adult in on the plan all along and
participating by agreement.

SHADES OF THE EVERLASTING COVENANT

Based on these clues, it seems clear that Abraham and Isaac were acting out a prophecy wherein another Father would later give His only Son as an offering for sin on the very same spot. As with Abraham and Isaac, this Father and Son would be doing so by prior agreement—in this case, one made before the foundation of the world was laid. And as God provided an innocent ram to die in place of Isaac, so He would provide the innocent Lamb of God, Who would die in our place. It makes sense then that Abraham named the location **Jehovah Jireh** meaning *on the mountain of the Lord it will be provided.* Because it was—on that very place.

Now you know the adult version.

CHAPTER TEN

ISAAC AND REBECCA: THE GOSPEL IN GENESIS PART TWO

WHAT IS THE MODEL FOR US IN THIS ANCIENT MARRIAGE?

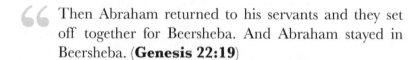

> Then Abraham returned to his servants and they set off together for Beersheba. And Abraham stayed in Beersheba. (**Genesis 22:19**)

Students have puzzled over this verse. Abraham had told his servants that he and Isaac would return to them (verse 5), and the Lord had provided a substitute offering sparing Isaac (verse 13) so why doesn't the verse say that Isaac also returned with Abraham? The answer is hidden in plain sight in chapter 24 when Isaac re-appears and completes the story of the Gospel in Genesis.

In **Genesis 24:1** we read that Abraham was now old and the Lord had blessed him in every way. Sarah had died, and Abraham had buried her in Hebron (**Genesis 23**), so he sent the chief servant in his household to the home of his relatives to choose a wife for Isaac, traditionally a mother's privilege. Abraham instructed him not to get Isaac a bride from the Canaanites, nor was he to take Isaac back to his homeland. If the woman he chose refused to come, then the servant was released from his duty **(Genesis 24:1-9)**.

WILL YOU MARRY HIM?

The servant packed 10 camels with gifts and set out for the town where Nahor, Abraham's brother, lived. When he arrived at the well outside the town, he asked the Lord to reveal to him the bride He had chosen for Isaac. As people came to gather water, the servant prayed that he would know which girl the Lord had chosen by asking her for a drink. If she gave him a drink and offered to help water his camels as well, she would be the one the Lord had selected for Isaac. Drawing enough water for 10 camels is no small task, so this would be a real sign. Before he had finished praying, Rebekah came along, and when he asked her for a drink, she agreed and offered to water his camels as well. The servant confirmed that she was from the family of Nahor (she was his granddaughter) gave her gifts, and asked to spend the night with the family.

Upon arriving at her family home, the servant told his story and formally asked for Rebekah on behalf of Isaac. Her family gave their permission, but the final decision was hers. When the servant explained they would need to leave immediately, she agreed to go—without hesitation—and they set off **(Genesis 24:10-61)**.

 Isaac had come in from the desert to Beer Lahai Roi one evening, and as he looked up in the distance, he saw them coming and went out to meet them. Rebekah spotted him and asked the servant who he was. "He is my master," the servant replied, so she covered herself with a veil as was the custom. Isaac brought her into the tent of his mother Sarah and married her, and she brought comfort to Isaac after his mother's death. **(Genesis 24:62-67)**

THE WELL OF LIVING WATER

This might be the best model of the relationship between the Father, the Son, Israel, and the Church in Scripture. Remember, from the command to offer his only son as a sacrifice, Isaac was as good as dead to Abraham. Three days later Abraham received Isaac back from death when the Lord provided a substitute sacrifice (**Genesis 22:4-6, 13 & Hebrews 11:17-19**). At this point, Isaac disappeared from the story. Abraham returned home with the servants for the burial of his beloved Sarah and sent an unnamed servant to the land of his family to obtain a bride for Isaac. The bride is supernaturally identified to the servant, given gifts by him, and must decide immediately to leave her familiar life. She then embarks upon a journey of unknown duration, with the servant as her guide, to marry a husband she has never seen. Isaac is re-introduced into the story on a day and hour previously unknown to the bride. They finally meet face to face near Beer Lahai Roi and they are married. Roughly translated, **Beer Lahai Roi** means *well of living water*.

GOD IS OUR COMFORTER

After God the Father had received His Son back from death, Jesus ascended into Heaven and disappeared from Earth. Later the Father presided over the death and burial of His beloved Israel. He also sent an unnamed Servant into the Earth in search of a bride for His Son. This Servant, The Holy Spirit, is called The Comforter by Jesus in **John 16:7** KJV but is known by no other name.

Although Abraham's servant is not named in **Genesis 24**, a few chapters earlier he is identified as **Eliezer** a name that roughly translates *God is our comforter* (**Genesis 15:2**).

The Holy Spirit seeks out supernaturally identified people (He knew us before the foundation of the Earth was laid) asking us to become the Bride of Christ, investing us with gifts when we agree (**Ephesians 1:13-14 & 1 Corinthians 12:7-11**).

We must decide immediately to leave our familiar life, and embark upon a spiritual journey of unknown duration, with the Comforter as our guide, to marry a husband we have never seen. On a day and hour previously unknown to us, our Betrothed will come out to meet us (**1 Thessalonians 4:16-17**). The Holy Spirit will usher us into the presence of the true Well of Living Water, and upon meeting Him face to face for the first time, we will wed.

Now you know the adult version.

CHAPTER ELEVEN

JACOB AND ESAU

ANOTHER MODEL OF THE MESSIAH?

Abraham's son Isaac had married Rebekah, and though they wanted children, Rebekah was unable to conceive. Isaac prayed to the Lord and she became pregnant—with twins!

> The babies jostled each other within her, and she said, "Why is this happening to me?" So she went to inquire of the Lord. The Lord said to her, "Two nations are in your womb, and two peoples from within you will be separated; one people will be stronger than the other, and the older will serve the younger."
>
> When the time came for her to give birth, there were twin boys in her womb. The first to come out was red, and his whole body was like a hairy garment; so they named him Esau. After this, his brother came out, with his hand grasping Esau's heel; so he was named Jacob. Isaac was sixty years old when Rebekah gave birth to them.

The boys grew up, and Esau became a skillful hunter, a man of the open country, while Jacob was a quiet man, staying among the tents. Isaac, who had a taste for wild game, loved Esau, but Rebekah loved Jacob.

Once when Jacob was cooking some stew, Esau came in from the open country, famished. He said to Jacob, "Quick, let me have some of that red stew! I'm famished!" (That is why he was also called Edom.)

Jacob replied, "First sell me your birthright."

"Look, I am about to die," Esau said. "What good is the birthright to me?" But Jacob said, "Swear to me first." So he swore an oath to him, selling his birthright to Jacob. Then Jacob gave Esau some bread and some lentil stew. He ate and drank, and then got up and left.

So Esau despised his birthright. (**Genesis 25:22-34**)

BORN CONTENDERS

These brothers were contentious from the beginning. Esau, whose name means *hairy*, was born a few minutes before Jacob, whose name means *conniver or schemer*. Easu was also called Edom, or *red*, from the color of the lentil stew for which he traded his birthright. That's the name he gave to his descendants, the Edomites, who settled the area northeast of the Dead Sea in today's Jordan. The Herods, who ruled over Israel in Roman times, were from Edom.

Esau and Jacob belong to the line of sons born to the patriarchs. Their lives showcase the Lord's ability to regain with a younger son, losses incurred by the firstborn—losses that could have damaged or destroyed man's hope for redemption. It's a model of man's second chance.

THE FIRSTBORN

A firstborn son had special rights and responsibilities. He was the official Kinsman Redeemer, responsible for preserving the family's assets. It was his responsibility to buy back what a family member had lost or mortgaged, and to purchase their freedom in cases of debt that led to slavery (**Leviticus 25:25**). He was also the Avenger of Blood. Since there was no organized law enforcement in those days, the firstborn was also responsible for seeing that those who caused the shedding of family blood paid their just penalty (**Numbers 35:19**). Eye for eye, tooth for tooth, limb for limb and life for life. He served as head of the family in the absence of his father. It was such an important position that his reward for assuming this responsibility was a double share of his father's estate.

LOST BY ONE, REGAINED BY THE OTHER

But for one reason or another, several firstborn sons either lost or gave up their position in favor of a younger one. Think of Cain and Seth, where Seth re-established the connection to mankind's redeemer broken by Cain's murder of Abel. Or Ishmael and Isaac, where Isaac remained the supernaturally born son of the promise even though Abraham and Sarah jumped the gun by appointing a surrogate mother to birth Ishmael. And Esau thought so little of his position as firstborn that he sold it to Jacob for a bowl of stew and earned the Lord's condemnation.

 "Was not Esau Jacob's brother?" the LORD says. "Yet I have loved Jacob, but Esau I have hated, and I have turned his mountains into a wasteland and left his inheritance to the desert jackals." Edom may say, "Though we have been crushed, we will rebuild the ruins." But this is what the LORD Almighty says: "They may build, but I will demolish. They will be called the Wicked Land, a people always under the wrath of the LORD. You

> will see it with your own eyes and say, 'Great is the
> LORD—even beyond the borders of Israel!'"
> **(Malachi 1:2-5)**

In fact, Jacob became so much more prominent than his brother
that the order of names has been reversed in referring to them, just
as God had told Rebekah before their birth. The contention
between them never completely went away. And as Moses was
leading the Israelites up the King's Highway from Egypt toward
Jericho, several hundred years later, the Edomites refused them any
water even though Moses offered to pay for it. Much later, under
King David, Israel conquered Edom completing the fulfillment of
the Lord's prophecy to Rebekah. And today, while Israel is once
again center stage in the world, Edom long ago ceased to exist as a
people.

Of course, the ultimate case to which all these first-born sons point
is Adam, the first son of God (**Luke 3:38**) who lost planet Earth
and all his descendants, and Jesus Who regained it all and more
(**Romans 5:12-19**).

OUR KINSMAN REDEEMER

Jesus came to Earth with obligations as both Kinsman Redeemer
and Avenger of Blood and had to be all God and all Man to fulfill
them. To regain the property Adam had lost, He had to buy it back.
To redeem Adam's progeny from their bondage of sin, He had to
pay off our debts. This was the responsibility of the Kinsman
Redeemer, and the required currency for both transactions was the
blood of a sinless man.

As the Avenger of Blood, He had to bring Adam and Eve's
murderer to justice. Remember, they were immortal until they
sinned. When Satan disputed God's warning that eating the
forbidden fruit would cause their deaths, he was lying. By
persuading them to disobey God, Satan orchestrated their demise
and was responsible for their deaths. Only someone with all the

authority and power of God could subdue such a powerful adversary. Our Lord Jesus fulfilled both roles at the cross.

HE PAID ALL OUR DEBTS

> When you were dead in your sins and in the uncircumcision of your sinful nature, God made you alive with Christ. He forgave us all our sins, having canceled the charge of our legal indebtedness, which stood against us and condemned us; he has taken it away, nailing it to the cross. And having disarmed the powers and authorities, he made a public spectacle of them, triumphing over them by the cross. (**Colossians 2:13-15**)

Turning what Satan believed was his greatest victory into his total defeat, Jesus made a public spectacle of him. By His one act of sacrifice, He purchased a complete pardon for all who would accept it, releasing them forever from the bondage of sin. Since that time, He waits for His enemies to be made His footstool because by one sacrifice He has made perfect forever those who are being made holy (**Hebrews 10:13-14**).

HE REDEEMED PLANET EARTH

> The creation waits in eager expectation for the children of God to be revealed. For the creation was subjected to frustration, not by its own choice, but by the will of the one who subjected it, in hope that the creation itself will be liberated from its bondage to decay and brought into the freedom and glory of the children of God. (**Romans 8:19-21**)

AND HE SEALED SATAN'S DESTINY OF DEFEAT IN THE
SPIRITUAL REALM

We await only the signal from God that the time has come, to
witness his capture and death in the physical realm.

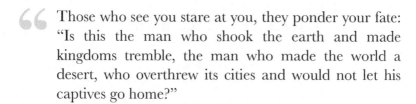

> Those who see you stare at you, they ponder your fate:
> "Is this the man who shook the earth and made
> kingdoms tremble, the man who made the world a
> desert, who overthrew its cities and would not let his
> captives go home?"
>
> All the kings of the nations lie in state, each in his own
> tomb. But you are cast out of your tomb like a rejected
> branch; you are covered with the slain, with those
> pierced by the sword, those who descend to the stones
> of the pit. Like a corpse trampled underfoot, you will
> not join them in burial, for you have destroyed your
> land and killed your people. (**Isaiah 14:16-20**)

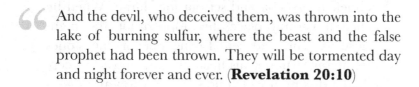

> And the devil, who deceived them, was thrown into the
> lake of burning sulfur, where the beast and the false
> prophet had been thrown. They will be tormented day
> and night forever and ever. (**Revelation 20:10**)

Now you know the adult version.

CHAPTER TWELVE

JACOB'S LADDER

AND STILL ANOTHER MODEL OF THE MESSIAH?

66 Jacob left Beersheba and set out for Haran. When he reached a certain place, he stopped for the night because the sun had set. Taking one of the stones there, he put it under his head and lay down to sleep. He had a dream in which he saw a stairway resting on the earth, with its top reaching to heaven, and the angels of God were ascending and descending on it. There above it stood the LORD, and he said: "I am the LORD, the God of your father Abraham and the God of Isaac. I will give you and your descendants the land on which you are lying. Your descendants will be like the dust of the earth, and you will spread out to the west and to the east, to the north and to the south. All peoples on earth will be blessed through you and your offspring. I am with you and will watch over you wherever you go, and I will bring you back to this land.

I will not leave you until I have done what I have promised you."

When Jacob awoke from his sleep, he thought, "Surely the LORD is in this place, and I was not aware of it." He was afraid and said, "How awesome is this place! This is none other than the house of God; this is the gate of heaven." (**Genesis 28:10-17**)

HOW DO YOU EXPLAIN THAT?

Jacob—his name means *conniver*—tricked his father Isaac into giving him the blessing intended for his twin brother Esau. Esau swore to kill Jacob, so their mother warned him to flee to her family's home in Paddan Aram, some distance away. "When your brother calms down," she told him. I'll send for you." (**Genesis 27:44-45**)

He was near Shiloh, a little north of the place that would become Jerusalem. This was where the tabernacle stood when the Israelites first came into the Promised Land, and where a growing number of scholars today believe the Millennial Temple will stand. As Jacob dreamt of the stairway leading from Earth into Heaven the Lord spoke to him, renewing the covenant He had made with Abraham (**Genesis 15**) and then Isaac (**Genesis 17:19**).

In each case it was clear. The covenant was unconditional—a free gift to Abraham's descendants. Abraham had neither asked for it nor was any compensation ever mentioned (although Joshua learned that to actually occupy the land, the Israelites would have to dispossess the indigenous residents.)

The locals were a 10-nation confederacy of pagan tribes. The Lord had given them 400 years to repent of their idolatry and return to Him. Since they had ignored His warnings, He brought the Israelites to act as His agency of judgment against them. And just so the Israelites would know the outcome was never in doubt, the Lord went before them to frighten and weaken their enemies, stopping the

Jordan's flow, tearing down their walls and even making the Sun and Moon stand still in the sky. In fact, the only casualties the Bible records in the whole campaign came from the Battle of Ai, where the Israelites were disobedient to God and thereby deprived of His help.

WE'RE A LITTLE AHEAD OF OUR TIME

But this was all still several centuries in the future when the Lord spoke to Jacob in his dream. What Jacob knew was that he stood on Holy Ground. As he prepared to continue on his journey, he named the place **Bethel**, which means *House of God.*

Nearly 20 centuries later Jesus, recalling Jacob's dream, identified Himself as the stairway on which the angels of God were ascending and descending (**John 2:51**). In doing so, He declared that He was the bridge between Heaven and Earth, spanning the awful chasm between them caused by sin's entry into the world.

BUT WAIT, THERE'S MORE

And not only that. Just as He explained that the stairway was symbolic of Him, He also showed that the place Jacob had named Bethel was symbolic of the nation Israel. For though Bethel is indeed located in the Promised Land, it's really the descendants of Jacob who are the "House of God." They are His people, and it was through them that the Messiah Redeemer had come to be our Stairway to Heaven. For in the bargain, God opened His house to the Gentiles as well (**Galatians 3:26-29**).

Because of his dream, Jacob thought he had stumbled onto some mysterious portal to another world, the "Gate of Heaven." But later Jesus would claim that the gate stood for Him as well. "I am the gate; whoever enters through Me will be saved." (**John 10:9**)

Heaven and Earth were once unified, and the only will was God's will. Then sin entered the world through Satan's great deception and with it came man's loss of immortality. Access to the Garden was forbidden, but an angel was stationed at its entrance, "guarding the way to the Tree of Life" signifying that one day man would again become immortal.

But first, that awful chasm that had separated man from God would have to be bridged. The Lord chose the Jewish people to be His own and through them brought forth the Messiah to accomplish just that. With His shed blood the Messiah built a stairway to Heaven, and with His death became the gate. All who enter through Him (believing His death purchased a pardon for their sins) whether Jew or Gentile would become immortal, climb the Stairway to Heaven and dwell in the House of God forever.

Now you know the adult version.

CHAPTER THIRTEEN

JOSEPH AND HIS COAT OF MANY COLORS

HOW MANY TIMES DO YOU HAVE TO TELL US?

> Joseph, a young man of seventeen, was tending the flocks with his brothers, the sons of Bilhah and the sons of Zilpah, his father's wives, and he brought their father a bad report about them. Now Israel (Jacob) loved Joseph more than any of his other sons because he had been born to him in his old age; and he made an ornate robe for him. When his brothers saw that their father loved him more than any of them, they hated him and could not speak a kind word to him. **(Genesis 37:2-4)**

You know the story. Joseph was his father Jacob's favorite son. Jacob didn't try to hide this from his other sons, and he gave an extravagant robe to Joseph only.

Joseph then had two dreams. In one, he and his 11 brothers were represented by sheaves of wheat. During the dream, their sheaves all bowed down before his. In the other, the sun, moon and 11 stars were all bowing before him. His father interpreted this to mean that these celestial bodies represented him, Joseph's mother, and the 11 brothers. This further incensed his brothers, making their rejection complete. One day when Jacob had sent Joseph to find his brothers and see how they were doing, they conspired against him, captured him, and threw him into a pit. Then they sold him to slave traders bound for Egypt. They faked his death, showing their father his fancy robe all covered in blood as evidence of Joseph's untimely demise. As far as Jacob was concerned, his beloved son was dead.

YOU CAN'T KEEP A GOOD MAN DOWN

Arriving in Egypt, Joseph was purchased by Potiphar, the captain of Pharaoh's guard, and quickly rose to a position of trust in his household. Angered because Joseph refused her sexual advances, Potiphar's wife had him thrown into jail on false charges. Again, he rose to a prominent position, overseeing the entire prison operation. While there, he interpreted the dreams of two prisoners and when his interpretations proved correct, he was called to the attention of Pharaoh, who had also had a disturbing dream. Joseph interpreted this dream as a prediction of seven good harvest years to be followed by seven years of famine so severe they would wipe out all the gains of the good years and then some.

Pharaoh appointed Joseph, a man without station or influence, to devise a strategy to save the people from this famine and made him the number two authority in all Egypt, subject only to Pharaoh. During the good years, Joseph married the daughter of an Egyptian priest. And by successfully implementing his strategy when the famine came, Joseph saved them all from certain death, enabling Pharaoh to take possession of Egypt and all its wealth in the process.

WHAT THEY INTENDED FOR EVIL, GOD INTENDED FOR GOOD

When the famine reached the land of Canaan, Jacob sent his sons to Egypt to purchase food. While purchasing food from him, they didn't recognize the brother they had sold into slavery. Joseph put his 11 brothers through a series of disastrous events to place them entirely at his mercy, and then eventually revealed his true identity and offered them his forgiveness. He explained how God had turned their evil into good. After a highly emotional reunion, Jacob and the 70 members of his family were given the most favored land in Egypt. By the way, Joseph's dreams did come true. Jacob and his wives, and the 11 brothers and their wives, and all their children bowed down before Joseph, who had saved them all and brought them into a land of plenty where they enjoyed generations of peace and prosperity.

THE OLD TESTAMENT COMES ALIVE

Parables are Heavenly truths put into Earthly context, and the Bible abounds with them. The ones Jesus told are mostly stories He devised for the purpose, but the Lord told Paul that He often orchestrated real life events in Israel to help teach us about Him (**Romans 15:4 & 1 Corinthians 10:11**). In this story, Jacob and his family represent Israel, Joseph the Messiah, and Pharaoh God the Father. Joseph's Gentile Bride is the Church and Egypt the world. The seven good years are the Age of Grace during which the Gentile Bride is taken, the seven bad years the Tribulation period where the Messiah is revealed to Israel. The land of Goshen is the Kingdom Age. Put the Heavenly Players in place of the Earthly ones to gain the lesson and see the Old Testament come alive as never before.

TELL ME A STORY, DADDY

Although our Lord Jesus was sent by His Father to His brothers to see to their well-being, they rejected Him, conspiring against Him and causing His death. He was consigned to Hell, sold as a slave to sin. He had no Earthly station or influence but was appointed to save the world from sin. He was given a position of prominence on Earth receiving all power and authority subject only to the will of His Father. By successfully implementing His strategy, He saved us all from certain death, enabling His Father to regain possession of the world and all its wealth in the process. After taking a Gentile Bride, He will put His brothers through a series of disastrous events contrived to place them entirely at His mercy and permit the revelation of His true identity. A highly emotional reunion will result in Israel again receiving the most favored land in all the Earth where they will enjoy 1,000 years of peace and prosperity.

We've just scratched the surface here. There are over 100 clear truths being modeled in the life of Joseph. The rest is up to you.

Now you know the adult version.

CHAPTER FOURTEEN

MOSES, THE PRINCE OF EGYPT

HOW DID GOD PREPARE MOSES TO BECOME ISRAEL'S LEADER?

> As the sun was setting, Abram fell into a deep sleep, and a thick and dreadful darkness came over him. Then the Lord said to him, "Know for certain that for four hundred years your descendants will be strangers in a country not their own and that they will be enslaved and mistreated there. But I will punish the nation they serve as slaves, and afterward they will come out with great possessions. You, however, will go to your ancestors in peace and be buried at a good old age. In the fourth generation your descendants will come back here, for the sin of the Amorites has not yet reached its full measure."

When the sun had set and darkness had fallen, a smoking firepot with a blazing torch appeared and passed between the pieces. On that day the Lord made a covenant with Abram and said, "To your descendants I give this land, from the Wadi of Egypt to the great river, the Euphrates—the land of the Kenites, Kenizzites, Kadmonites, Hittites, Perizzites, Rephaites, Amorites, Canaanites, Girgashites and Jebusites." (**Genesis 15:12-21**)

As the story of Joseph ended, the family of Israel had been relocated into Egypt and given its finest land in return for the incredible services Joseph had performed in saving all Egypt, while vastly enriching Pharaoh. So how did Egypt's honored guests become despised slaves by the time Moses was born?

WHAT HAVE YOU DONE FOR ME LATELY?

The explanation, from **Exodus 1:8-22**, was summarized by Stephen as he reviewed Israel's history before the Sanhedrin.

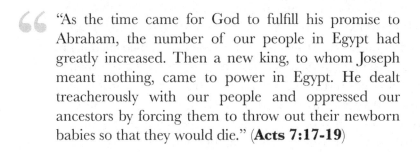 "As the time came for God to fulfill his promise to Abraham, the number of our people in Egypt had greatly increased. Then a new king, to whom Joseph meant nothing, came to power in Egypt. He dealt treacherously with our people and oppressed our ancestors by forcing them to throw out their newborn babies so that they would die." (**Acts 7:17-19**)

Four hundred years is a long time to remember anything, especially when Egyptian life spans were only about 35 years long. Also remember, within one generation, the children of Israel had forgotten all about the miracles associated with their arrival in the Promised Land. They had forgotten, even though elaborate attempts were made to help them remember, and it had been one of their greatest victories (**Judges 2:10**).

Over 10 Egyptian generations had passed, and the family of Israel had grown to more than one million people. They were now a feared and hated minority. There's also an indication from the

Greek language of **Acts 7** that Egypt's then current ruler was not from the same family as the Pharaoh of Joseph's time, and maybe not even Egyptian.

Into this environment, Moses was born. By Jewish tradition, his mother had a vision that her baby boy would redeem his people. That's why she went to such extremes to protect him from the edict that brought death to all Jewish infant boys. And it explains why she floated him down the river in a basket, to be retrieved by Pharaoh's daughter. And so Pharaoh provided a home, education, and military training for the one who would ultimately bring about his downfall.

FOUR HUNDRED YEARS OR FOUR GENERATIONS, WHICH IS IT?

Scoffers note the apparent conflict between 400 years and four generations in God's promise to Abram. Read it carefully against the backdrop of ensuing passages, and you'll find that there were indeed 400 years from Abram to Moses, and there were also four generations from Moses until the Israelites settled in the Promised Land. The length of a generation is measured by the span of time from a man's birth until the birth of his first son—in Biblical times, about 40 years. Moses lived through three of these. He was about 40 years old when he fled to Midian after killing an Egyptian soldier, 80 when he returned to confront Pharaoh, and 120 when he died on Mount Nebo just across the Jordan from the Promised Land. The generation of Israelites who crossed the Jordan and conquered the land were the fourth generation since the parents of Moses learned of his impending birth and role as Israel's deliverer.

From the third generation who left Egypt with Moses, all but two—Joshua and Caleb—perished in the desert as a consequence of their disobedience, (**Deuteronomy 1:35**) leaving their children to inherit the land.

I believe Moses knew from his mother's vision that he was Israel's deliverer. This helps explain his behavior when he killed an Egyptian for beating a Hebrew slave—and then criticized a fellow

Hebrew for doing the same thing (**Exodus 2:11-14**). He was acting in his own strength to begin their deliverance, but the slave responded, "Who made you ruler and judge over us?" God had a better plan, but now His chosen one was a murderer and fugitive from the law. God's grace abounds even in sin, so Moses found refuge in the desert while those in Egypt either died or forgot him.

When he returned, the Prince of Egypt was a nobody shepherd from Midian, acting in the strength of the Lord. And though Pharaoh called himself a god, Moses was now more than a match for him. While each of the ten plagues was aimed at one of the gods of Egypt, the last one—the death of the firstborn—was reserved for the man who called himself god.

As for the ten nations of Canaan whose land God had promised to Abraham's descendants, their sin was now complete. After 400 years of waiting in vain for them to repent and return to Him, the One who made them and loved them had run out of patience. Soon His armies would cross the Jordan and exact the punishment God always demands of those who refuse His grace and mercy (**Deuteronomy 18:9-13**). Israel would fight the only war of aggression in their entire history and receive the land He promised them as their everlasting reward.

Now you know the adult version.

CHAPTER FIFTEEN

THE PASSOVER: EXODUS 12

WHAT WAS THE GREATEST MIRACLE OF THE PASSOVER?

Let's review: the descendants of Israel had been in Egypt nearly 400 years, and toward the end of that time were greatly oppressed. The Pharaoh in charge now didn't remember how Joseph had saved Egypt and made it the most powerful nation on Earth (**Acts 7:18**). The Pharaoh was fearful of this foreign minority that seemed to be growing at an alarming rate. To help keep things under control, he brought in troops to force the Israelites into slavery, making bricks for his massive construction projects. Then he ordered their midwives to kill all the male babies as they were born. But they tricked him, and now one of those baby boys who should have died had grown up to become a powerful leader, demanding that Pharaoh set them free.

Pharaoh thought himself a god, and was not about to give in to a mere man—a Hebrew slave at that. It took 10 plagues, supernatural judgments from the God of the Hebrews, to change his mind. The first nine plagues brought destruction on Egypt from which they never recovered, with most of their crops and livestock destroyed, their drinking water turned to blood, and their bodies racked with pain from infestation and disease.

But it was the tenth one that really did them in. Earlier, the Lord had told Moses what his final plague would be. "Israel is my first born son, and if you don't let my people go, I'll take your firstborn son." (**Exodus 4:22-23**). Now Moses angrily told Pharaoh what the fate of Egypt would be (**Exodus 11:1-10**).

THE PASSOVER

That day the Lord gave Moses special instructions for the Hebrews —and anyone else who wanted to be saved—to follow. On the 10th of the month, they were to select a year-old male lamb from among the flocks, one for each family. From the 10th till the 14th they were to inspect it carefully to be sure it was without defect or blemish. Then at twilight on the 14th, they were to slaughter the lamb and roast it over an open fire. They were to paint its blood on the doorpost and lintel of their homes.

When the lamb was ready, each family was to eat the meat along with some bitter herbs (horseradish) and some bread baked without yeast. Breaking no bones in the process and burning any leftovers, they were to eat standing up, packed and ready for a rapid departure. That same night, the destroying angel would come through Egypt to take every firstborn from among the families of Egypt. As he did, the destroying angel would look at the door of each home, and where he saw the lamb's blood, he would "pass over" that home sparing those inside. Where there was no blood, the firstborn would die. And so it was.

About midnight, the firstborn of every home not marked by the blood of the lamb died. During the remainder of the night, the Egyptians pleaded with the Hebrews to leave. Moses had instructed the Israelites to ask the Egyptians for gold, silver, and clothing, and the Egyptians gladly gave to them, wanting the Israelites to leave quickly. And from that day to this, the Passover is celebrated annually in every Jewish home in commemoration of that event.

CHRIST IN THE PASSOVER

Christians in growing numbers also celebrate the Passover today. We do so because of the unmistakable hints of the Messiah evident in the Passover Story. The Hebrews were saved by the blood of the lamb, but only after applying it over their doors. Obviously, Jesus is the true Lamb of God (**John 1:29**). And as it was with them, it isn't the sacrifice of the Lamb of God that saves us, but the application of His blood to the doorposts of our hearts.

In addition, as they painted each doorpost and lintel, they were unknowingly making the sign of the cross, down and across, down and across. They roasted lambs on a vertical spit with the lamb fastened upright by its forelegs to a cross bar on the spit, another clear model of the cross. And not just the Hebrews, but anyone in Egypt who applied the blood to their homes was saved.

On the morning of the 15th and for seven days thereafter, they ate unleavened bread, instituting the seven-day Feast of Unleavened Bread (**Exodus 12:15-17**). For the next seven days, the camp of Israel was rendered completely devoid of leaven. Leaven (we call it yeast) is a symbol of sin and seven the number of divine completeness. Ever since the true Lamb of God was sacrificed, all who apply His blood to their lives render themselves completely devoid of sin in God's eyes (**2 Corinthians 5:17-21**).

THE BIGGEST MIRACLE OF ALL

Taking the 600,000 men of military age (**Exodus 12:37**) and adding women, children, and the elderly, somewhere between 1.5 and 2 million Hebrews left Egypt that morning. No one was left behind. Think about that for a minute. 1.5 million people approximates the population of a fair sized city. What's the likelihood that in any city of that size, on any given day, all its inhabitants would be fit for a rigorous journey on foot? And don't forget, many of these people were overworked and undernourished slaves. Wouldn't sickness and injury be more likely among them than average folks? I believe the Lord supernaturally healed all their sick and injured that morning, probably the largest mass healing in human history.

And so the blood of the lamb did a lot more than just save them from the destroyer. The lame walked, the wounded were made whole, the sick were healed, the prisoners went free, the oppressed were released, and the poor became rich. Sounds just like what Jesus came to do for us.

Now you know the adult version.

CHAPTER SIXTEEN

CROSSING THE RED SEA

DID GOD REALLY BUILD A BRIDGE FOR THE ISRAELITES TO CROSS ON?

> When Pharaoh let the people go, God did not lead them on the road through the Philistine country though that was shorter. For God said if they face war they might change their minds and return to Egypt. So God led the people around by the desert road toward the Red Sea. (**Exodus 13:17-18**)

Tracing the route the Israelites took in their Exodus from Egypt has often caused confusion among students of this miraculous event. We'll use the Bible to help clarify things.

The easiest way to determine the route is to locate the various destinations mentioned, first the Red Sea itself and then, of course, Mount Sinai. For the Red Sea, let's have a look at **1 Kings 9:26.** "King Solomon also built ships at Ezion Geber which is near Elath in Edom on the shore of the Red Sea."

As you look at a map of Egypt, The Red Sea vaguely resembles the head of a rabbit whose ears define the Sinai Peninsula, called the Desert of Sin in Biblical times. The left ear is the Gulf of Suez and the right one the Gulf of Aqaba. Elath is modern Eilat on the northeast shore of the Gulf of Aqaba, on the border between Israel and Jordan. It's a beautiful resort famous for its bathing and diving due to the crystal-clear waters and warm temperatures. You can still see some of the pillars erected by King Solomon in nearby Ezion Geber.

Since the shores of the Red Sea are often steep and the waters very deep, the controversy over the location of the crossing stems partly from scholars' inability to find a convenient spot. This is compounded by an incorrect location for Mount Sinai and has led to a search for alternate places including the marshes of the Nile Delta region. None of these fit when compared with Biblical passages.

DID GOD REALLY SAY ... ?

Funny how our inability to understand God's ways will lead us to doubt His Word. We don't understand how He created the world in six days, so we assume He didn't and look for alternate explanations to support our assumptions. We don't understand how He can know the end from the beginning, so we assume He doesn't and spiritualize away the 40% of the Bible that is predictive prophecy. It seems like some scholars are forever telling us, "Here's what God really said," or "Here's what really happened."

But "My thoughts are not your thoughts neither are your ways my ways," declares the Lord (**Isaiah 55:8**). If God said something happened a certain way, it must be true, and if we search long and hard enough, we'll find confirmation. One of the great benefits of adhering to a literal interpretation of Scripture is discovering how well the Bible interprets and explains itself. When we seek Him with all our heart (**Proverbs 8:17**) and search the Scriptures diligently (**Acts 17:11**) we always find confirmation of His Word.

MT. SINAI—A CASE IN POINT

When Constantine converted to Christianity back in the early 300s, his mother Queen Helena did as well. Based on dreams she had, Helena went throughout the Middle East "locating" various Holy Places. Among them was Mount Sinai, which she placed in the Desert of Sin resulting in the region being called the Sinai Peninsula. Several facts from the Bible argue against this. First, the area is not a suitable encampment for the number of people Moses led out of Egypt (over one million). It lacks both sufficient space and a source of water. Second, though they spent years at the foot of Mt. Sinai, not a speck of evidence has ever been found to confirm their presence at Helena's location. Third, the Sinai Peninsula is in Egypt on the wrong side of the Red Sea, and from history we know that Egyptian troops regularly patrolled it due to mining operations they had there. In spite of this, for hundreds of years scholars have clung to her opinion. There's even a large monastery atop the mountain. Instead of concluding they had the wrong spot based on Biblical accounts, they've discounted the Word of God. And since they can't find supporting evidence where they're looking, some even doubt whether the event ever took place.

Meanwhile, on the other side of the Red Sea in Saudi Arabia, there's a mountain burned black on the top (**Exodus 19:18**) that Arabs have known about for centuries. It's called Jabal al Lawz or Jabal Mousa (Mountain of Moses). Nearby are the grave of Jethro, priest of Midian and father-in-law of Moses, (**Exodus 18:1**) and the springs of Elim with their 70 palms (**Exodus 15:27**). At the foot of this mountain, boundary pillars can be found (**Exodus 19:12**) along with an altar and an enormous split rock with a huge catch basin at its foot large enough to contain a small lake of fresh water (**Exodus 17:5-7**). There's even an Egyptian petroglyph depicting a golden calf. Saudi Arabia was once called Midian and is on the eastern side of the Red Sea across the water from Egypt right where Mount Sinai belongs. So now comes the question, how did they get across?

A BRIDGE UNDER TROUBLED WATERS

At the tip of the Sinai Peninsula, in the Gulf of Aqaba, there's a remarkable clue. The water is very deep all around, and the banks slope off sharply along most of its shoreline, but in the Straits of Tiran lies an abandoned freighter. Nearby there's a small beach area on both sides of the sea where it narrows considerably just at the entrance to the gulf.

This caught the attention of American explorer Bob Cornuke, who was there looking for the real Mount Sinai using Biblical accounts as his guide. Donning snorkeling gear, he headed into the crystal clear water for a closer look. As he stepped off the beach, he expected to descend rapidly into deep water like he had everywhere else along the coast. But here he found himself walking out into water that only gradually became deeper. This explained the presence of the abandoned freighter. It had run aground. The water is several hundred feet deep all around, but beneath the Straits of Tiran, there's an underwater land bridge connecting Egypt and Saudi Arabia, ancient Midian. The water covering this bridge, called Jackson Reef, never exceeds 40 feet in depth.

When God brought the Israelites here, Pharaoh thought he had them cornered. But the Creator of the Universe swept the waters back revealing the land bridge He had made just for this purpose. As Pharaoh's army pursued the Israelites, God let the waters roll back and drowned them all. A few days walk north on the eastern shore brought them to Mount Sinai in modern Saudi Arabia. From there it's a straight shot north skirting the land of Edom to the eastern shores of the Jordan across from Jericho.

Now you know the adult version.

CHAPTER SEVENTEEN

THE 10 COMMANDMENTS

WHAT IS THEIR REAL PURPOSE?

> And the Lord said to Moses, "Go to the people and consecrate them today and tomorrow. Have them wash their clothes and be ready by the third day, because on that day the Lord will come down on Mount Sinai in the sight of all the people." On the morning of the third day there was thunder and lightning, with a thick cloud over the mountain and a very loud trumpet blast. Everyone in the camp trembled. Then Moses led the people out of the camp to meet with God, and they stood at the foot of the mountain. Mount Sinai was covered with smoke, because the Lord descended on it in fire. The smoke billowed up from it like smoke from a furnace, and the whole mountain trembled violently. As the sound of the trumpet grew louder and louder, Moses spoke and the voice of God answered him. (**Exodus 19:10-11 & 16-19**)

In the following verses, God gave the children of Israel His 10 Commandments (not suggestions), basic laws that were later expanded into a total of 613 in the Torah (five books of Moses). In chapter 23, I will share my view that the giving of the Commandments was part two of God's four-part rebuttal to an accusation Satan had hurled at Him before the beginning of time. I have also noted the incredible similarity between the details surrounding the giving of the Law and the Rapture of the Church (read Moses, Jesus and the Rapture — on our website gracethrufaith.com).

When asked which were the greatest of all these laws, Jesus replied,

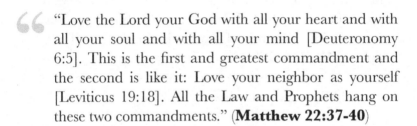

> "Love the Lord your God with all your heart and with all your soul and with all your mind [Deuteronomy 6:5]. This is the first and greatest commandment and the second is like it: Love your neighbor as yourself [Leviticus 19:18]. All the Law and Prophets hang on these two commandments." (**Matthew 22:37-40**)

The phrase *Law and Prophets* referred to the entire Old Testament, but those two commandments particularly summarize the ten given at Mount Sinai. The first four define how we should love the Lord our God (four is the number of Creation), and the last six how we demonstrate love for each other (six is the number of man).

GOD IS THE SAME, YESTERDAY, TODAY, AND FOREVER

Although He required the Israelites to obey His commandments, the Bible has said all along that they were given to expose the motives of man's heart and show his need for a Savior. God's standard is simply too high for sinful man to achieve. The Old Testament sacrifice of innocent animals pointed to this coming Savior. A Savior whose Blood alone would purchase their pardon and was meant to confirm their need for Him. The Lord Jesus made this abundantly clear in His Sermon on the Mount when He explained that even thinking about violating the Law is tantamount to doing so (**Matthew 5:21-22, 27-28**). He also made it clear that He hadn't come to abolish the Law but rather to fulfill it (**Matthew 5:17-18**). God's laws are still in force, we are still subject to them, and Jesus paid the ransom for our souls as well as theirs.

Throughout the Old Testament, the true purpose of the Law is explained. The prophet Micah asked,

> "With what shall I come before the Lord and bow down before the exalted God? Shall I come before Him with burnt offerings, with calves a year old? Will the Lord be pleased with 1000s of rams, with 10,000 rivers of oil? Shall I offer my firstborn for my transgression, the fruit of my body for the sin of my soul?" (**Micah 6:6-7**)

The Lord had Micah give this answer:

> "He has shown you, O man, what is good. And what does the Lord require of you? To act justly, and to love mercy and walk humbly with your God." (**Micah 6:8**)

Only by loving the Lord with all their heart and soul and mind and then loving their neighbors as themselves could they hope to accomplish this and no amount of external compliance with the Law could suffice in its absence.

King David, after committing adultery with Bathsheba and causing the death of her husband, prayed,

> Have mercy on me O God according to your unfailing love; according to your great compassion blot out my transgressions. Wash away all my iniquity and cleanse me from my sin. You do not delight in sacrifice or I would bring it; you do not take pleasure in burnt offerings. The sacrifices of God are a broken spirit. A

broken spirit and a contrite heart O God You will not despise. (**Psalm 51: 1-2 & 16-17**)

David admitted that he had broken the law. But he knew that with sincerity and humility he could ask for and receive forgiveness, and that God would prefer this to an empty gesture of sacrifice. The prophet Nathan later explained to David that he could be forgiven in Heaven, but that didn't necessarily relieve him of the Earthly consequences of his behavior (**2 Samuel 12:1-12**). (Those who run around saying, "I'm under grace, not the Law," would do well to remember this.)

EVERYTHING THAT WAS WRITTEN IN THE PAST WAS WRITTEN TO TEACH US (ROMANS 15:4)

The children of Israel had promised to do "everything the Lord has said" (**Exodus 19:8**). Yet before Moses could get down off the mountain with the 10 Commandments they had broken most of them. Centuries later Paul admonished us, "Therefore no one will be declared righteous in His sight by observing the Law, rather through the Law we become conscious of sin" (**Romans 3:20**). Just as a speed limit sign lets us compare our speed with the legal limit, the Commandments let us compare our behavior with God's requirements. When we're exceeding the speed limit, the sign prompts us to slow down. When we're not meeting God's requirements, the Law prompts us to seek forgiveness.

Now you know the adult version.

CHAPTER EIGHTEEN

AND THE WALLS CAME TUMBLIN' DOWN

WHO REALLY WON THE BATTLE OF JERICHO?

> On the tenth day of the first month the people went up from the Jordan and camped at Gilgal on the eastern border of Jericho. At that time the Lord said to Joshua, "Make flint knives and circumcise the Israelites again." On the evening of the 14th day of the month, while camped at Gilgal on the plains of Jericho the Israelites celebrated the Passover. The day after Passover, that very day, they ate some of the produce of the land; unleavened bread and some roasted grain. The manna stopped the day after they ate this food from the land. There was no longer any manna for the Israelites, but that year they ate of the produce of Canaan. (**Joshua 4:19, 5:2, 10-12**)

WATER WORKS

The crossing of the Jordan was at least as big a miracle as the crossing of the Red Sea. The Jordan River was at flood stage that spring, but the Lord stopped the flow of the river so that the water piled up upon itself and the whole nation crossed over on dry ground (**Joshua 3:13-17**). A column of people 400 abreast would have required all day to cross while the floodwaters piled up higher and higher. When the kings of the various tribes inhabiting the land heard about this "their hearts melted and they no longer had the courage to face the Israelites" (**Joshua 5:1**).

You have to admire the Lord's show of strength here. This ragtag army of desert nomads was closely watched as they arrived on the East Bank of the Jordan. No doubt, the Amorite kings felt secure since the flooding and swollen river separated them from this strange group. But the Lord, Who ordained the laws of nature in the first place, simply overruled one of them and caused the river to stop flowing. Imagine the looks on the faces of those watching this grand spectacle. And when they had crossed, did the Lord send them into battle formation and prepare them to face the fiercest enemy in all the land? No, they camped in full view of the enemy, enjoyed some of the produce of the land, *and had all their fighting men circumcised.*

Four days later, having healed somewhat, they celebrated Passover for only the third time in their history, and then they prepared for the coming battle. You have to suppose the inhabitants of Jericho just stood on the walls of their fortress and watched all this, too afraid to attack even while the Israelites were incapacitated. Makes me think of **Proverbs 16:7**: "When a man's ways are pleasing to the Lord, He makes even his enemies live at peace with him."

A MAN WITH A PLAN

 Now when Joshua was near Jericho, he looked up and

saw a man standing in front of him with a drawn
sword in his hand. Joshua went up to him and asked,
"Are you for us or for our enemies?" "Neither", He
replied, "But as the commander of the army of the
Lord I have now come." Then Joshua fell facedown to
the ground in reverence and asked Him, "What
message does the Lord have for His servant?" The
commander of the Lord's army replied, "Take off
your sandals for the place where you are standing is
Holy." And Joshua did so. (**Joshua 5:13-15**)

Any doubt Joshua might have had about the identity of this Visitor
was erased when he heard the same command previously given to
Moses at the Burning Bush (**Exodus 3:4-6**). Here was the Son of
God in an Old Testament appearance, the Heavenly Joshua giving
the Earthly one his battle plan. And what a plan it was. (Joshua is
derived from the same Hebrew root as Yeshua, the Hebrew name
for Jesus.)

 Now Jericho was tightly shut up because of the
Israelites. No one went out, and no one came in.
Then the Lord said to Joshua, "See I have delivered
Jericho into your hands, along with its king and
fighting men. March around the city once with all the
fighting men. Do this for 6 days. Have 7 priests carry
trumpets of rams' horns in front of the Ark. On the
7th day march around the city 7 times with the priests
blowing the trumpets. When you hear them sound a
long blast on the trumpets, have all the people give a
loud shout; then the city wall will collapse and the
people will go up, every man straight in." (**Joshua
6:1-5**)

And so it was. At the sound of the trumpets on the seventh day, and
the seventh time around, the people shouted, and the walls fell
down. The Israelites marched in and destroyed every living thing in

the city: the people, the animals, and all their possessions. The city was put to the torch, and a curse pronounced over its ashes.

SPIRITUAL WARFARE

This battle was a Spiritual one. Joshua and the army of Israel were only along for the ride. The Lord wasn't on their side—they were on His. The first six times around the city was to show that with man alone the victory would be impossible (6 is the number of man, incomplete without God). The final seven showed that with God all things are possible. 6 (man) + 1 (God) = 7 (complete). The total of 13 circuits represents the apostasy of the inhabitants of Jericho that brought this judgment upon them. Thirteen is the number of apostasy or rebellion.

Remember the Lord's promise to Abraham. "Know for certain that your descendants will be strangers in a country not their own and they will be enslaved and mistreated 400 years. But I will punish the nation they serve as slaves, and afterward they will come out with great possessions. You however will go to your fathers in peace and be buried at a good old age. In the fourth generation your descendants will come back here for the sin of the Amorites has not yet reached its full measure." (**Genesis 15:13-16**)

Then there's the Lord's admonition to Israel in the desert before they crossed the Jordan, "When you enter the land the Lord your God is giving you, do not learn to imitate the detestable ways of the nations there. Let no one be found among you who sacrifices his son or daughter in the fire, who practices divination or sorcery, interprets omens, engages in witchcraft, or casts spells, or who is a medium or spiritist, or who consults the dead. Anyone who does these things is detestable to the Lord and because of these detestable practices the Lord your God will drive out those nations before you" (**Deuteronomy 18:9-12**).

In the only war of aggression Israel has ever fought, they were agents of God's judgment against a people who had known the Lord but abandoned Him for pagan idols. Having given them over

400 years to repent of their detestable practices and return to Him, He finally ran out of patience and brought judgment against them.

Referring to the people living in the land, He commanded the Israelites, "Do not leave alive anything that breathes" (**Deuteronomy 20:16-18**). In describing the conditions there, He had said, "Even the land was defiled, so I punished it for its sin and the land vomited out its inhabitants (**Leviticus 18:25**). Had the Israelites been faithful to this command, many of the problems they face today would have been avoided (**Judges 2:1-3**).

Now you know the adult version.

CHAPTER NINETEEN

THE GOSPEL IN JOSHUA: THE STORY
OF RAHAB

HOW IS RAHAB THE HARLOT A MODEL OF THE CHURCH?

The similarities between the Books of Joshua and Revelation are striking. In fact, some call Joshua a model for Revelation, particularly when it describes the battle of Beth Horon in chapter 10.

The Israelites were confronted by a coalition of five Amorite kings led by someone who called himself Adoni-zedek, or Lord of Righteousness (a model of the anti-christ?). There were signs in the sun and moon as in **Revelation 6:12, 8:12**, and **16:8-11**, and large hailstones fell from the sky as in **Revelation 8:7** and **16:21**. The five Amorite kings hid in caves for fear of the Israelites just as in **Revelation 6:15** the kings of the Earth will hide in caves for fear of the wrath of the Lamb.

At the end of Joshua, the land is dispossessed of its usurpers, at the end of Revelation the Earth is dispossessed of its usurpers and as I indicated in the previous chapter, the name Joshua is derived from the same Hebrew root as Yeshua, the Hebrew name for Jesus. But to me, the most dramatic similarity is hidden in the story of Rahab. Hence the title of this chapter.

THE GOSPEL IN JOSHUA

As the Israelites gathered along the east bank of the flooded and swollen Jordan, they were closely watched by the people of Jericho, only a short distance from the river's western shore. They had heard how the Lord had parted the Red Sea to allow the Israelites to escape the Egyptian army, and how He had helped them to utterly defeat the two Amorite kings east of the Jordan. In Rahab's own words, "When we heard of it our hearts melted and everyone's courage failed because of you for the Lord your God is God in Heaven above and Earth below." (**Joshua 2:11**). Then the people of Jericho stood aghast as the God of Israel stopped the flow of the raging river, allowing His people to cross on dry ground.

When Joshua sent two spies into Jericho, they found their way to Rahab's home and sought refuge there, which she granted in return for their guarantee of safety for her and her family. They agreed and told her that if she marked her home with a scarlet cord, she and anyone in the house with her would be spared in the coming battle (**Joshua 2:12-21**). On the day of battle, the city was captured, and everyone within its walls died, except for Rahab and her family. She had gathered her family in her home and marked it with the scarlet cord as they had agreed. Before burning the city to the ground, Joshua had the two spies go to Rahab's home and bring her and all her family out to dwell among the Israelites (**Joshua 6:22-25**).

By the way, can you picture this? Her house was built into the city wall, which came tumbling down at the shout of the Israelite army. Of all the massive stonework protecting the city of Jericho, only that portion containing the home of Rahab was left standing. What a witness to the power of God, who "knows how to rescue Godly men from trials, and to hold the unrighteous for the Day of Judgment." (**2 Peter 2:9**) (See also **1 Thessalonians 1:10**)

BY GRACE WE ARE SAVED, THROUGH FAITH

The name **Rahab** means *proud*, but among the people of Jericho, all of whom knew of the God of Israel, only Rahab humbled herself before the two spies and confessed Him as "God in Heaven above and Earth below." And speaking of the spies, what about them? Except for reporting that all the people of Jericho were scared to death did the spies bring Joshua any intelligence that helped develop the battle plan? No. The Lord had already determined the battle plan, and they contributed nothing to it (**Joshua 6:2-5**). So what was their true purpose in His plan? It seems like they were really two witnesses sent to hear Rahab's confession, save her from destruction, and give her a place among the Lord's people.

From that time on, Rahab dwelt with the Israelites. She married a man from the tribe of Judah named Salmon and had a son whom they named Boaz. Boaz took a Gentile Bride from Moab named Ruth, and they had a son named Obed, who had a son named Jesse, who had a son named David, who became King of Israel (**Ruth 4:13-22**). And 26 generations later, two distant cousins who were both descendants of King David (and therefore of Rahab and Salmon) married and became the Earthly parents of our Lord Jesus. And so when you read the genealogy of Jesus in Matthew, you'll find Rahab listed there (**Matthew 1:5**).

IT'S NOT WHAT YOU KNOW, BUT WHO YOU KNOW THAT MATTERS

Everyone in Jericho had heard about the God of Israel and all but Rahab and her family were destroyed on the day of battle. Rahab's faith saved her. When she believed in her heart that only One Who is God in Heaven above and Earth below could have done the things she had heard about, He went to great lengths to reveal Himself to her, sending two witnesses to testify of His power and love.

Immediately after confessing Him as God, she was:

- Marked with a sign that guaranteed her security (**Ephesians 1:13-14**),
- Called out from all the others in Jericho (**Romans 8:29-30**),
- Hidden on the day of battle (**Isaiah 26:20-21 & Revelation 3:10**),
- And brought alive into the family of the Redeemer (**1 Thessalonians 4:16-17**).

Just like we are.

Now you know the adult version.

CHAPTER TWENTY

SAMSON AND DELILAH

WHY DID SAMSON'S STRENGTH GO AWAY WHEN HIS HAIR WAS CUT?

> A certain man of Zorah, named Manoah, from the clan of the Danites, had a wife who was sterile and remained childless, unable to give birth. The angel of the Lord appeared to her and said, "You are barren and childless, but you are going to become pregnant and give birth to a son. Now see to it that you drink no wine or other fermented drink and that you do not eat anything unclean. You will become pregnant and have a son whose head is never touched by a razor because the boy is to be a Nazirite, dedicated to God from the womb. He will take the lead in delivering Israel from the hand of the Philistines." (**Judges 13:2-5**)

The woman gave birth to a boy and named him Samson (*sunshine*). He grew and the Lord blessed him, and the Spirit of the Lord began to stir in him while he

was in Mahaneh Dan, between Zorah and Eshtaol.
(**Judges 13:24-25**)

The story of Samson is one of the most famous of the children's
Bible stories because Samson was a real-life superhero—the world's
first. We all know how he killed a lion with his bare hands (**Judges
14:6**) slew 1,000 Philistines with the jawbone of an ass (**Judges
15:14-16**) and wound up in the clutches of Delilah (her name
means *languishing*) (**Judges 16**). She betrayed him to the Philistines
by convincing him to tell her the secret of his strength. As soon as
they knew his weakness, they shaved his head, gouged out his eyes,
and imprisoned him. Later, at a great feast honoring their god
Dagon for helping them capture Samson, they brought him out of
prison to perform for them. He had his guard lead him to a place
between the central pillars of the stadium, and asking the Lord for
strength, pushed the pillars over, collapsing the whole building and
killing himself and all the Philistine leaders (**Judges 16:23-30**). No
Saturday morning cartoon ever had more drama, action, and
victory over seemingly overwhelming odds.

HAIR TODAY, GONE TOMORROW

But the story becomes even more fascinating when we search the
Scriptures for clues to its deeper meaning. In **Numbers 6:1-8** the
Lord gave Moses directions on the proper way to execute a special
vow of separation called the Nazirite vow. As the angel had
instructed Samson's parents, people taking the Nazirite vow could
not cut their hair, drink any wine, or partake of any food or drink
derived from grapes. Normally the vow was voluntary, and kept for
a period of time to demonstrate a commitment to God, after which
the person returned to a normal life. But three times in Scripture
the Lord designated a yet to be born child as a lifelong Nazirite. All
three were born to previously barren women: Samson, Samuel (**1
Samuel 1**) who anointed David as Israel's king, and John the
Baptist (**Luke 1**), who proclaimed the coming Messiah. Our Lord

Jesus, by the way, was a Nazarene (from Nazareth) but not a Nazirite.

So have you figured out why Samson's supernatural strength failed when Delilah betrayed him to the Philistines and they shaved his head? That's right, Samson violated his Nazirite vow by revealing it and therefore allowing his hair to be shaved. His commitment to the Lord was broken and his strength gone because "the symbol of his separation to God is on his head" (**Numbers 6:7**). While *languishing* in prison, he recommitted himself and grew his hair back, permitting the Lord to restore his supernatural power for one last feat of strength, fulfilling his life's purpose to begin Israel's deliverance from the Philistines (**Judges 13:5**).

WHERE IS PALESTINE?

As an aside, the Philistines pronounced their name with a hard P, not with the soft PH or F sound we're used to, making it sound more like Palestine. When the Romans conquered Israel, they renamed the land Palestine (Land of the Philistines) on their maps as an insult to the Jews. This insult has continued through the centuries, and that's why some call Israel Palestine to this day. The Romans were just one of a long line of Gentile nations refusing to acknowledge Israel's right to the land, but some Palestinians use this connection with the Philistines as a basis for a claim to the land predating the arrival of Joshua and the Israelites.

IS THAT YOU LORD?

But back to our story. Earlier, Manoah had inquired of the Angel of the Lord, "What is your name so that we may honor you when your word comes true?" He replied, "Why do you ask my name? It is beyond understanding." (**Judges 13:17-18**) The Hebrew word **pele** translated *beyond understanding* in the NIV is rendered *Wonderful* in the King James. It's the same word used in **Isaiah 9:6**.

> For unto us a child is born, and unto us a son is given
> and the government will be upon His shoulders. And
> He will be called Wonderful (pele), Counselor, Mighty
> God, Everlasting Father, Prince of Peace.

I think Isaiah used these five titles to hint that the Messiah would personify the Trinity, being all God and all man. Mighty God and Everlasting Father are self-evident, and Counselor is the name given the Holy Spirit in **John 14:25**. Prince of Peace always refers to the Lord Jesus, and I believe Wonderful refers to Him as well. Five, the number of grace, indicates that the Messiah came to demonstrate God's Grace. If I'm right, the angel appearing to Manoah was the Lord Jesus in one of His many Old Testament appearances.

But to me, the most remarkable lesson is the way in which Samson's life parallels the history of Israel. Both were set apart from birth, foretold by an angel, called to begin the deliverance of God's people, and supernaturally empowered against overwhelming odds. Both sought after strange women (false gods) and were blinded for disobedience, but finally called upon the Lord, and brought judgment upon His enemies.

Now you know the adult version.

CHAPTER TWENTY-ONE

DAVID AND GOLIATH

WHY DID DAVID PICK UP FIVE STONES, WHEN ONE WAS ENOUGH?

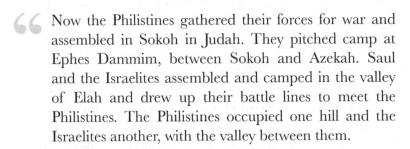

Now the Philistines gathered their forces for war and assembled in Sokoh in Judah. They pitched camp at Ephes Dammim, between Sokoh and Azekah. Saul and the Israelites assembled and camped in the valley of Elah and drew up their battle lines to meet the Philistines. The Philistines occupied one hill and the Israelites another, with the valley between them.

A champion named Goliath, who was from Gath, came out of the Philistine camp. His height was six cubits and a span (over nine feet). He had a bronze helmet on his head and wore a coat of scale armor of bronze weighing 5,000 shekels (125 lbs.), on his legs he wore bronze greaves (shin guards), and a bronze javelin was slung on his back. His spear shaft was like a weaver's rod, and its iron point weighed 600 shekels (15 lbs.). His shield bearer went ahead of him.

Goliath stood and shouted to the ranks of Israel, "Why do you come out and line up for battle? Am I not a Philistine and are you not servants of Saul? Choose a man and have him come down to me. If he is able to fight and kill me, we will be your subjects. But if I overcome him and kill him, you will become our subjects and serve us."

Then the Philistine said, "This day I defy the ranks of Israel. Give me a man and let us fight each other."

On hearing the Philistine's words, Saul and all the Israelites were dismayed and terrified. For 40 days the Philistine came forward every morning and every evening and took his stand. (**1 Samuel 17:1-11, 16**)

AND A LITTLE CHILD SHALL LEAD THEM

David was the youngest of the eight sons of Jesse. The three oldest had followed Saul to war. And as was the custom of the time, David, being too young to enlist, carried food and other supplies to his brothers in support of the war effort.

One morning he arrived at the Israelite camp in time to hear Goliath's daily challenge to the men of Israel. "Who is this uncircumcised Philistine that he should defy the armies of the Living God?" he demanded (**1 Samuel 17:26**). Even though the prophet Samuel had already visited Jesse's home and anointed David as Israel's next King, (**1 Samuel 16:13**) to his brothers, he was still a little kid who had come to embarrass them, and they tried to send him home.

But King Saul heard of David's questions and sent for him. David said to Saul, "Let no one lose heart on account of this Philistine, your servant will go out and fight him." (**1 Samuel 17:32**) When Saul reminded David that he was just a boy, David recalled the times while tending sheep when the flock had been attacked by both bear and lion, and David had defeated them. "The Lord Who delivered me from the paw of the lion and the paw of the bear will deliver me from the hand of this Philistine," he declared. Saul said to David, "Go, and the Lord be with you." (**1 Samuel 17:37**)

We all know how David, armed with only a slingshot, fired a stone into Goliath's forehead and killed him. And how the Israelites chased the Philistine army all the way back to the gates of their cities, completing Israel's deliverance from Philistine bondage, a task Samson had begun earlier (**Judges 13:5**). But as exciting as this story is on the surface, there is even more hidden beneath.

LESSONS IN THE OLD TESTAMENT

Several times in Scripture, the Lord informs us of the value of these stories from Israel's history (**Romans 15:4 & 1 Corinthians 10:11**). We're to learn the lessons they contain, not just repeat them as historical accounts. They were orchestrated to reveal truths about God, and none more so than the story of David and Goliath.

If you see the story as a parable on spiritual warfare, you'll gain some remarkable insight. The word **parable** means to *lay along side* so we're not discarding the historical validity of the account, just gaining another level of understanding.

The main characters in Biblical parables always represent someone or something else, so try seeing Goliath and the Philistines as Satan and his demonic host, Saul and the Israelites as people in the flesh, and David as people in the Spirit.

For 40 days, Saul and his army were intimidated and paralyzed by the defiant words of Goliath, just as in the flesh, people are intimidated and paralyzed by the power of Satan. Forty is the Biblical number of testing, and shows that in the flesh we will always fail against the enemy. And as David discovered, not even the king's own armor, the best they could fashion, was suitable protection but instead further encumbered and immobilized him (**1 Samuel 17:38-39**).

Our struggle is not against flesh and blood, but against the rulers, against the authorities, against the powers of this dark world, and against the spiritual forces of evil in the Heavenly realms (**Ephesians 6:12**). For though we live in the world, we do not wage war as the world does. The weapons we fight with are not the weapons of the world. On the contrary, they have divine power to demolish strongholds (**2 Corinthians 10:3-4**).

Wearing Saul's armor, David was an awkward and ineffective boy, but armed in the strength of the Lord he was more than a match for the giant Goliath (**1 Samuel 17:45-47**). "Not by might, nor by power, but by My Spirit," says the Lord Almighty (**Zechariah 4:6**).

LOGIC VS. EMOTION

It's good to remember that there was logic to David's position and not just emotion. Sure, he was indignant at Goliath's defiance of the Lord's Army and angry that no Israelite had accepted the challenge, but the Lord had already used him to defeat a lion and a bear, either of which could have been a match for Goliath. And he had been anointed as Israel's next king, an unconditional promise God could not fulfill if David was defeated and killed. So David had his own past experience and the promise of One who cannot lie to bolster his faith. Knowing these things, he didn't believe the possibility of defeat existed (**1 Samuel 17:32-37**).

Parables have often been described as Heavenly stories put into an Earthly perspective. To gain their wisdom, just put things back into the spiritual realm. Doing so, we find that we have the same logical support for our faith that David had for his. The Lord has already defeated His enemy and ours (**Colossians 2:15 & 2 Timothy 1:10**) and we've been promised not only kingship (**Ephesian 2:6-7**) but also sonship (**Galatians 4:4-5**) by the one who cannot lie. These are unconditional promises that God cannot fulfill if we can be overcome and defeated by our enemy. Knowing these things, we can't logically believe the possibility of defeat exists. Fear and faith cannot dwell in the same mind at the same time. Submit yourselves then, to God. Resist the devil and he will flee from you (**James 4:7**) just as the Philistines fled from the Israelites.

By the way, when David went out to face Goliath he stooped down and picked up five smooth stones (**1 Samuel 17:40**). Ever wonder why? It turns out Goliath had four brothers (**2 Samuel 21:18-22 KJV**).

Now you know the adult version.

CHAPTER TWENTY-TWO

ELIJAH ON MOUNT CARMEL

WHY DID ELIJAH DOUSE THE ALTAR THREE TIMES?

> So (King) Ahab sent word throughout all Israel and assembled the prophets on Mount Carmel. Elijah went before the people and said, "How long will you waver between two opinions? If the Lord is God follow Him, but if Baal is God follow him." (**1 Kings 18:20-21**)

A LITTLE BACKGROUND PLEASE

As King David's life was drawing to a close, the Lord chose his son Solomon to succeed him. It was the time of Israel's closest approximation to the Messianic Kingdom promised by God. There was peace in the land, and Israel's influence in the world was without equal. Kings from every land came and paid homage to Solomon, whose wisdom was legendary. Solomon reigned in peace and prosperity for 40 years, but toward the end of his reign he began to pay the price for his one act of disobedience. The Lord had forbidden the Israelites from marrying foreign women, knowing that they would bring pagan gods into Israel and lead their husbands into false religion (**1 Kings 11:2**).

In violation of the Lord's prohibition, Solomon had taken 700 wives and 300 concubines, many of them foreign. He had permitted them to worship their own gods, even building idols of some on a hill east of Jerusalem. This angered the Lord and caused a civil war in Israel that resulted in the Kingdom being divided. Following the death of Solomon, the Northern Kingdom, called Israel, which included the land given to 10 of the 12 tribes, descended rapidly into idol worship while the smaller Southern Kingdom, called Judah, which included the land given to the remaining two tribes, remained faithful to God.

During this time, all those in the Northern Kingdom who remained faithful to God migrated south with the Levites (**2 Chronicles 11:16**) so all the 12 tribes were represented in the Southern Kingdom. The notion of 10 tribes being lost following the subsequent defeat of the Northern Kingdom by Assyria is not Scriptural, and any doctrine based on the so-called lost 10 tribes is therefore suspect. But that's a topic for another day.

HOW LONG WILL YOU WAVER BETWEEN TWO OPINIONS?

For the next 80 years, the people of the Northern Kingdom vacillated between allegiance to God and allegiance to various Canaanite deities—sometimes worshipping all of them at the same time. During Elijah's time, there had been a drought in Israel for three years, a sign of God's displeasure with this ongoing flirtation with paganism. Ahab was King of Israel and had married a daughter of the King of neighboring Phoenicia (Lebanon), a powerful and influential woman named Jezebel. She personally supported 450 prophets of Baal and 400 prophets of Asherah. It was these prophets that Ahab summoned to Mount Carmel in response to Elijah's "invitation." In the presence of all the people, Elijah (his name means *God is Lord*) had challenged the prophets of Baal to a contest designed to reveal the one true God.

 Elijah said to them, "I am the only one of the Lord's prophets left, but Baal has 450 prophets. Get two bulls for us. Let Baal's prophets choose one for themselves, and let them cut it into pieces and put it on the wood but not set fire to it. I will prepare the other bull and put it on the wood but not set fire to it. Then you call on the name of your god, and I will call on the name of the Lord. The god who answers by fire—He is God." Then all the people said, "What you say is good." (**1 Kings 18:22-24**)

All that morning the prophets of Baal called upon their god. They danced around their altar, and cut themselves with knives, part of their religious practice. At noon Elijah began to taunt them. "Shout louder," he said, "Surely he is a god. Perhaps he is relieving himself or busy or traveling. Maybe he is sleeping and must be awakened" (**1 Kings 18:27**). This went on all through the day with no response from Baal. Then at the time of the evening sacrifice, Elijah took 12 stones, one for each of the 12 tribes of Israel, and built an altar for the Lord. He dug a trench around it and placed wood upon it. He cut the other bull into pieces and arranged them on the wood. Then he had the people bring four large jars filled with water that they poured on the offering and the wood. "Do it again," he said, and they did. "Do it a third time," he ordered, and they did. The water ran down around the altar and filled the trench. And then he prayed. "O Lord, God of Abraham, Isaac and Israel, let it be known today that You are God in Israel, and that I am your servant and have done all these things at your command. Answer me O Lord, answer me, so these people will know that You O Lord are God and that You are turning their hearts back again." (**1 Kings 18:36-37**) Talk about a grandstand play. Can't you just feel the tension mounting each time the altar was doused?

Then the fire of the Lord fell and burned up the sacrifice, the wood, the stones and the soil and even licked up the water in the trench. When the people saw this they fell prostrate and cried, "The Lord— He is God. The Lord—He is God" (**1 Kings 18:39**). Elijah had them seize the pagan prophets and execute them according to Mosaic law (**Deuteronomy 13:1-5**) and shortly thereafter, rain fell on the land of Israel for the first time in three years, a sign of God's pleasure. Jezebel swore out a death curse on Elijah but God took him alive into Heaven. The people later abandoned God again, judgment came in the form of the Assyrian armies, and the Northern Kingdom ceased to exist.

YOUR MISSION, SHOULD YOU CHOOSE TO ACCEPT IT

At the close of the Old Testament, the Lord promised that Elijah would return to Earth to herald the coming Messiah. He would once again turn the hearts of the fathers to their children and the hearts of the children to their fathers, or else God would strike the land with a curse (**Malachi 4:5-6**). Jesus said that John the Baptist was the promised Elijah (**Matthew 17:11-13**), and although the hearts of many were turned to God, King Herod put him to death. Thirty-eight years later, the land was struck with a curse, judgment came in the form of the Roman armies, and the Nation Israel ceased to exist.

At the end of the age, Elijah will once again bring drought upon the Earth at the Lord's command, and for the third time will implore the people to repent of their sins, and again, the hearts of many will be turned to God. The antichrist will think he's put him to death, but again God will take him live into Heaven (**Revelation 11:11-12**). Judgment will come in the form of the Lord's armies and the world, as we know it, will cease to exist.

THIS IS YOUR LAST CHANCE

Elijah used four jars of water to douse the altar three times. Four is the number of the earth (by the end of the fourth day its creation was complete), and the water can represent the pouring out of the Holy Spirit (see **John 7:37-39**). If so, then the three dousings of the altar hint at Elijah's three missions to Earth, offering God's Holy Spirit and imploring the people to turn their hearts back to Him. After limited success, each one ends in failure and is followed by a judgment. Each time, the Lord in His mercy provides His people another chance.

The Millennium is man's last chance; there is no fourth mission for Elijah. But at the end of the Millennium, in spite of utopian conditions with Satan bound and 1,000 years of personal rule by the Lord Jesus Himself, there's still enough residual evil in the heart of unregenerate people for Satan to mount a rebellion as soon as he's freed (**Revelation 20:7-10**). This illustrates man's total inability to remain faithful to God. In spite of 7,000 years of history filled with the undeniable revelations of God's existence and His endless patience in dealing with us, only the shed blood of Jesus is able to make us fit to dwell in His presence.

Now you know the adult version.

CHAPTER TWENTY-THREE

THE ADVERSARY PART ONE: THE SHINING ONE

WHERE DID SATAN COME FROM?

Let's pause in our series of the most well known children's stories to get a better look at the great adversary who stands behind every effort to thwart God's will in these events. He is a created being (**Ezekiel 28:13**) whose creation is not mentioned in the Genesis account. So we'll assume that he was created along with the other angelic beings, in the gap between **Genesis 1:1 and 1:2** (see Chapter 1, In the Beginning). All we know by way of introduction, is that he turns up in the Garden in the form of a **serpent** (the Hebrew means *enchanter*) to beguile our first parents. But from **Isaiah 14:12-20** and **Ezekiel 28:11-19** we can piece together a profile of this great adversary, his origin, fall, and destiny.

HOW YOU HAVE FALLEN FROM HEAVEN, O LUCIFER

His name comes from **Isaiah 14:12** (KJV). **Lucifer** is actually the Latin translation of a Hebrew phrase that means *to shine* in the sense of making a show or celebration or (foolish) boast and recalls the title "shining one." **Ezekiel 28:12-14** indicates he was created as "the model of perfection, full of wisdom and beauty" and anointed as the guardian cherub on the holy mount of God. In the Septuagint translation of the Hebrew Scriptures, all the stones contained on the breastplate of Israel's High Priest are listed in **Ezekiel 28:13** perhaps hinting at his responsibilities. Combining the Ezekiel and Isaiah passages, we can infer that he was head of the congregation of angelic beings, charged with leading them in the worship of the Almighty, and guardian of His Throne.

The "foolish boast" part of his name came to bear when wickedness was found in him (**Ezekiel 28:15**). Excessively proud of his beauty and wisdom, he rebelled against God and uttered his infamous "five I wills" culminating in a declaration that he would make himself "like The Most High" (**Isaiah 14:13-14**). This was the first of countless repetitions caused by the sin nature in people. This prompts people to emulate Lucifer, trying to become like God by exalting, glorifying and even deifying themselves. The next time it happened was in the Garden when Adam and Eve were deceived into thinking they could "become like God" (**Genesis 3:5**).

Satan's rebellion brought judgment upon him and the seat of his throne, Planet Earth, leaving it an uninhabitable ruin for who knows how long. As I've said, many believe this all took place in the apparent gap between the first two verses of Genesis. If so, it helps reconcile the conflict between a geologically proven old Earth (10 billion years) and the Biblically described young civilization (6,000 years). I should also note that recent measurements of the speed of light indicate that it may have been gradually slowing down over time. If that's proven true, then all our speculation about the age of Earth's ancient past goes out the window. But, again, that's another story.

SATAN IS ALIVE AND WELL ON PLANET EARTH

Hal Lindsey, is his book so titled, speculates that at his judgment Satan hurled two accusations at God: "You're not just and You have no love." In response to these accusations God did the following:

1. He created people, beings vastly inferior to the angels but sharing with them the properties of intellect, agency (power of choice) and eternal life, and gave them dominion over Planet Earth.

2. He gave us a set of rules to live by and ordained that obedience to them was a requirement for life. Any violations (sins), even those committed only in the mind, would be punishable by death. There were no loopholes, and no one would escape judgment. **Perfect justice**.

3. He sent His Son to live a life in total compliance with these rules, the only man ever to do so, granting Him the right to govern the universe and receive all its worth as His inheritance.

4. He gave His Son's life to purchase a pardon for sin—decreeing that all who accept His death as payment for their sins will receive eternal life and share in this inheritance as His adopted children. **Perfect love.**

WHAT DO YOU SAY TO THAT?

Satan's response to God's first action was to immediately steal control of Planet Earth and cause the contamination of the human gene pool with a sin nature. This sin nature we inherited after the fall makes it impossible for us to obey God's rules, condemning us all to death. And then, he used all his powers of deception to try and prevent us from ever learning about the pardon God had purchased for us. Or failing in that, to trick us into thinking we don't qualify, by infiltrating the Church (**2 Corinthians 11:13-15**) to promote his false doctrine (**Galatians 1:8, Colossians 2:8, 1 Timothy 4:1**). In that way, he thinks he can cause so many to be condemned that God, out of His love for us, will have to bend His rules and overlook our sins. If He bends for man, He'll have to bend for Satan.

Satan is the god of this age (**2 Corinthians 4:4**), and the prince of this world (**John 12:31, 14:30, 16:11**), having the whole world under his control (**1 John 5:19**). But the deceiver has deceived himself. Too proud to turn to God, he thinks to defeat Him (foolish boast), even though his own defeat was determined at the cross (**Colossians 2:13-15**). While the Holy Spirit currently restrains his authority over Earth (**2 Thessalonians 2:5-8**—see also Who is the Restrainer), during the Great Tribulation, he'll be free to do his worst. But it won't be enough. And having been expelled from Heaven (**Revelation 12:7**), he'll be bound in the Abyss for 1,000 years (**Revelation 20:1-3**) and finally cast into the eternal fire (**Revelation 20:10**).

Now you know the adult version.

CHAPTER TWENTY-FOUR

THE ADVERSARY PART TWO: I WILL MAKE MYSELF LIKE THE MOST HIGH

WHO OWNS PLANET EARTH?

> How you have fallen from heaven, O Lucifer son of the dawn. You have been cast down to the earth, you who once laid low the nations. You said in your heart, "I will ascend to heaven. I will raise my throne above the stars of God. I will sit enthroned on the mount of the assembly, on the uttermost heights of the sacred mountain. I will ascend above the tops of the mountains. I will make myself like the Most High." (**Isaiah 14:12-14**)

WHAT'S GOING ON HERE?

Was the one we call Satan trying to replace God or become a god himself? The key lies in the term "Most High." It's used for the first time in **Genesis 14:18-19**, where God is described as the Most High God, possessor of Heaven and Earth (KJV). Some of the modern translations substitute creator or maker for possessor, but the Hebrew favors the KJV. Normally **bara**, which means *to create* is used in referring to the Creator but in **Genesis 14:19** it's **qanah**. Qanah appears 82 times in Scripture and although it can mean create, it's not translated that way anywhere else in Scripture. It literally means *to get or acquire* and implies ownership.

Everything in the universe belonged to the One who had created it, and some speculate that He had permitted Satan to place his throne here on Earth. After all, Satan was an important dignitary among the principalities and powers in the Heavenly realms (**Ezekiel 28:14 & Jude 8-10**). But although he wasn't the creator of Heaven and Earth, he didn't want to be a mere tenant. He wanted to own the place outright and become a parallel focus of worship (becoming like the Most High) so he rebelled against God causing the judgment we discussed last chapter.

POSSESSOR OF HEAVEN AND EARTH?

This view makes the subsequent actions by both God and Satan more easily understood. Ever wonder why, in all the six days of creation, the only work God did not pronounce as good was on the second day, the creation of the Heavens (**Genesis 1:6-7**)? Remember there are three locations in the Bible called *Heaven*—the Earth's atmosphere, the vast reaches of space beyond, and the throne of God. The Hebrew word used in **Genesis 1:1** and **Genesis 6-7** (KJV) is unusual in that it's a dual form, like our word *both*. It can only include two of whatever is being referenced, in this case, **Heavens**. So it describes our *atmosphere, and space beyond*, omitting God's Throne.

That same Hebrew word for **Heaven** is used in **Genesis 14:19**. And in **Ephesians 2:2** Paul refers to Satan as the "ruler of the kingdom of the air." The Greek word there means *atmosphere*. Could it be that upon the creation of the Heavens Satan and his fellow rebels immediately invaded them, preventing God from taking pleasure in that which He had just made? If so, Satan became the possessor of "Heaven" at that time (squatter's rights?). This also explains why when Paul refers to being "caught up to Paradise" (**2 Corinthians 12:2-4**) he takes pains to call it the third Heaven, God's Throne.

Then, when God created Adam and gave him dominion over the Earth, Satan's response was to steal it from him—since he had failed to get it from God, and become the possessor of Earth (**1 John 5:19**). In the wilderness temptation, one of the things Satan offered our Lord was the authority and splendor of all the kingdoms of Earth (**Matthew 4:8-9**). You can't give what you don't own, and the Lord did not dispute Satan's claim of ownership.

AT THE CROSS

The Lord's mission to Earth was clearly foretold in the Old Testament. Satan knew that along with redeeming Adam's descendants, regaining ownership of planet Earth was a primary objective. That's why he was willing to negotiate it away in the wilderness temptation. After all, if Jesus agreed, Satan would still have the Heavens and could still be worshiped, even by the Son of God. But the Lord refused, and then at the cross something happened that Satan hadn't foreseen at all (**Colossians 2:13-15**). All of Adam's progeny could now choose to become God's children, the sin problem having been overcome, and those who refused would do so by choice, relieving God of any responsibility for them. Satan's chance to use unsaved humanity as leverage to save himself had disappeared.

THE SECRET RAPTURE

And check this out. Soon, at a date and hour still undisclosed, those who have chosen to become God's children will meet the Lord in the air (first Heaven) (**1 Thessalonians 4:16-17**). (Does the Lord intend the Rapture of the Church as a sneak attack to begin repossessing the Heavens?) Then at the beginning of the Great Tribulation, Satan will be expelled from the second Heaven (**Revelation 12:12**). And finally, at the Second Coming, the Lord will set up His kingdom here, having defeated Satan's armies. Now, who's the possessor of Heaven and Earth?

Surely this is why our Creator—the master of strategy—kept the Rapture of the Church secret until after the cross, completing the conversion of what Satan foresaw as a huge victory into his utter defeat. It's also why Paul was able to declare that none of the "rulers of this age" understood this in advance, for if they had, they would not have crucified the Lord of Glory (**1 Corinthians 2:8**). Jesus spoke not a word of the Rapture to his disciples, but had Paul introduce it after it was too late for the enemy to react. It was a secret component of the Lord's strategy to entirely reverse Satan's bid to become possessor of Heaven and Earth.

Now you know the adult version.

CHAPTER TWENTY-FIVE

THREE BOYS IN THE FIERY FURNACE

WHERE WAS DANIEL?

After Assyria had conquered the Northern Kingdom in 722 BC, all that was left of Israel was a small portion around Jerusalem called Judah. In spite of the judgment experienced by their cousins in the north, Judah also fell into a state of idolatry, and so the Lord permitted Babylon to conquer them as well (**Jeremiah 25:8-9**). In his first siege of Jerusalem in 605 BC, the King of Babylon took hostages from the Royal family to ensure the king (that he left in place as a vassal) would govern Judah according to his wishes. This plan was ultimately unsuccessful, and so in 586 BC after two more sieges, he completely destroyed Jerusalem including the Temple Solomon had built and carried off all its inhabitants into slavery.

Among the royal hostages were Daniel, a future prophet of Israel whom the King renamed Belteshazzar, and three friends, Hananiah, Mishael, and Azariah renamed Shadrach, Meshach, and Abednego. These four were given training and education in the ways of Babylon and prepared to serve the King in his court (**Daniel 1:1-7**). They proved to be excellent students. And within a few years, following Daniel's interpretation of a dream that had troubled the

King, were appointed to positions of administrative authority over the Province of Babylon (**Daniel 2**).

YOU SHALL HAVE NO OTHER GODS BEFORE ME

Some time later, King Nebuchadnezzar decided to have a giant golden statue of himself placed in a prominent place on the plains of Dura outside the city. It was 60 cubits (90 ft.) tall, six cubits wide, and—according to tradition—stood on a pedestal six steps high. And here you have the first clue of what's really going on in this children's story (666). The King required all his subjects to bow down and worship the statue and decreed that anyone refusing to do so would be thrown into a fiery furnace and burned alive (**Daniel 3:1-7**). It should also be noted that the pagan rites of worship in Babylon included public acts of a sexual nature.

Shadrach, Meshach, and Abednego had maintained their covenant relationship with the God of Israel and refused to bow down and worship anyone other than Him, especially since it included behavior that was forbidden under God's law. This act of disobedience was reported to the king and, though fond of them, he was furious. He offered them a second chance to comply with his command. They rejected it, saying that their God was able to rescue them, but even if He didn't they still would worship no one else. So he had them bound and thrown into the furnace (**Daniel 3:16-23**) as he had threatened to do.

Apparently, this furnace was constructed in a public place (so the punishment could be witnessed by all) because the king saw his three disobedient subjects in the fire. But he was shocked to see a fourth figure in there as well— one who looked like "the Son of God," and all four were walking around in the fire unbound (**Daniel 3:25**). King Nebuchadnezzar called Shadrach, Meshach, and Abednego to come out of the furnace, and to his utter amazement discovered that they were totally unharmed, not even the smell of smoke on their clothing. The only things burned up were the ropes that had bound them. The king gave praise to the God of Israel and decreed that from that time on anyone who said anything against Him would be executed "for no other god can save in this way" (**Daniel 3:28-29**).

TYPES AND SHADOWS

In addition to recounting an actual event from Israel's history and being a favorite of children for ages, this story is a prophecy of a time yet future to us. One day soon, another world ruler will make an image of himself and require that everyone in the world bow down and worship before it, on pain of death (**Revelation 13:13-18**). The King of Babylon, therefore, becomes a model for the antichrist, and the fiery furnace represents the Great Tribulation. Shadrach, Meshach, and Abednego foreshadow the remnant of Israel preserved through the judgment (**Revelation 12:13-14**) and freed from the bondage of their religion for a closer walk with their Messiah (**Zechariah 12:10-11**).

ANY QUESTIONS?

Where was Daniel during this? This question often goes unasked. Daniel and King Nebuchadnezzar had developed a special relationship starting from the time he had interpreted the king's dream. It was at Daniel's suggestion that Shadrach, Meshach, and Abednego were given positions of responsibility (**Daniel 2:49**). He was their benefactor and, like them, had remained faithful to his covenant with God. Yet he appears nowhere in this story. Daniel is one of only two Biblical characters about whom nothing critical is ever said (the other is Joseph), so it's unlikely that he bowed down and worshiped the statue. And since he had humiliated the other "wise men" in the King's court by being the only one who could interpret the King's dream, it's also hard to believe that they would let him get away with disobeying the King's command.

The only plausible explanation is that Daniel had gone away during this time, and perhaps it was his absence that gave the others the courage to report Shadrach, Meshach, and Abednego for their non-compliance. If so, then Daniel becomes a remarkable type of the Church—whose disappearance before the Tribulation begins removes us from the time and place of judgment, (**Revelation 3:10**) releases the restraint against evil in the world, (**2 Thessalonians 2:7**) and begins the time of Israel's greatest persecution (**Matthew 24:21**).

You can't base a pre-Tribulation Rapture doctrine on this, but if you're already so inclined, the story of the three boys in the fiery furnace takes on added meaning. It becomes another one of those beautiful models the Lord has built to instruct and encourage us with events from Israel's history. For everything that was written in the past was written to teach us, so that through endurance and the encouragement of the Scriptures we might have hope (**Romans 15:4**).

Now you know the adult version.

CHAPTER TWENTY-SIX

THE HANDWRITING ON THE WALL

WHO WROTE IT AND WHAT DID IT MEAN?

Daniel was an old man in his eighties, and retired from public service, when he received the urgent message to report immediately to the Great Banquet Hall in Babylon—the city where he and his fellow Jews had been captive for nearly seventy years.

The Babylonian king, Nebuchadnezzar, had died some years before, his son, the current king, was away in a remote part of the kingdom, and so his grandson, Belshazzar was in charge. Daniel had become a close friend and advisor to Nebuchadnezzar but didn't much care for his grandson. The feeling was mutual.

Although a massive army of Medes and Persians were camped outside the city wall, inside, there was a party going on. In spite of the massive enemy force—or maybe to taunt them—Belshazzar had thrown this party for a thousand of his closest friends and their dates. The intent was to project a feeling of security inside the city while demoralizing the enemy troops outside.

Even without this attempt at psychological warfare, Babylon was a formidable challenge to any army. The city was 14 miles on a side, with walls 350 feet high and 87 feet thick. At strategic points along the walls, hundreds of lookout towers rose an additional 100 feet into the desert air. The wide thoroughfare that ran along the top of the city wall was the scene of periodic chariot races, with sometimes as many as four chariots abreast racing at full speed for the prize.

The mighty Euphrates River ran through the city bringing all the fresh water they could use, and fields and pastureland inside the walls assured a steady supply of food. The Babylonians could survive in their fortress city indefinitely.

On top of that, huge bronze grated gates were lowered down into the river where it flowed under the city walls to deprive any would-be enemy access from the water. So the people had good reason to feel safe, hence the celebration. They thought the city was impregnable.

As the party progressed and the wine flowed ever more freely, someone called for a toast, and soon everyone was thanking and praising the Babylonian gods they credited with protecting them. And as a further affront to the God of the Hebrews, Belshazzar called for the cups and goblets his grandfather had looted from the Temple in Jerusalem, and placed in the Babylonian museum, to use in toasting their pagan gods. It was certainly a festive mood.

Suddenly, the fingers of a human hand appeared and wrote on the plaster wall behind the King's head, near the lampstand in the royal palace. The king watched the hand as it wrote. His face turned pale, and he was so frightened that his knees knocked together, his legs gave way, and according to some renderings of the passage, he soiled his undergarments (**Daniel 5:5-6**).

That immediately changed the mood. In the blink of an eye, the place was as quiet as a church on Monday morning. Belshazzar called for his magicians and promised that anyone who could read the writing would become the third highest in the Kingdom, next to his father and himself. But no one could. Belshazzar was terrified now. This hand appearing out of nowhere had been bad enough, but having written something no one could understand made it even worse. Who did this and what did they want?

Then Belshazzar's grandmother, the widow of Nebuchadnezzar, hearing all the fuss came into the hall and suggested they find the old Hebrew Prophet Daniel. She remembered how he had interpreted her husband's dreams years ago. Maybe he could solve this puzzle, too.

So Daniel was located and brought into the hall. When he saw the writing, he understood it immediately and wasted no kindness or diplomacy on this boy who would be king. When offered the third spot in the hierarchy, he said: "You may keep your gifts and give your rewards to someone else, nevertheless I will read the writing and tell you what it means." (**Daniel 5:17**)

Then he reminded Belshazzar how incredibly powerful his grandfather had been, how the God of the Hebrews had put even him in his place, and how he'd been humbled by the experience. "But you, Belshazzar have not humbled yourself even though you knew all this." And he proceeded to chastise Belshazzar publicly for his arrogance and pride (**Daniel 5:22-24**).

Then he read the handwriting on the wall. It turns out it was written vertically, and the columns ran right to left. And as with all Aramaic, the vowels had to be assumed from the context. Without knowing the context it was next to impossible to insert the correct vowels, so between that and the vertical writing, everyone was confused. Daniel understood because God gave him the insight.

The first two letters M and N were repeated and stood for **mene, mene** or in English *number, number*. The next column to the left read TKL. Adding the vowels gave him the word **tekel** or *weighed* in English. The final group of letters was PRS, and here Daniel inserted vowels and used the plural to make **parsin**. Using the two possible meanings of the word gave him *divided* and *Persians*.

So these were the words: **Mene, mene, tekel, parsin**. *Number,*

number, weighed, divided, Persians. With the wisdom of the Holy Spirit, Daniel translated it thus:

 "God has numbered the days of your reign and brought it to an end [literally your number is up]. You have been weighed on the scales and found wanting. Your kingdom is divided and given to the Medes and Persians."

In spite of his earlier protestations, Daniel was immediately made the third ruler of Babylon. Later that night the Medes and Persians stormed through the gates and captured the city. Belshazzar was slain, but the city and its inhabitants were spared. The prophecy had been fulfilled.

Nearly 200 years earlier, before the city of Babylon was built or the king he named was born, Isaiah had prophesied that Cyrus the Persian would conquer this fortress city and told how it would be done (**Isaiah 44:27-45:6**). The flow of the Euphrates would be temporarily diverted making the water level drop in Babylon and allowing a contingent of Persian soldiers to go under the bronze grates and open the city gates from the inside, thereby taking the city without a fight.

A few days after the Medo-Persian coalition captured Babylon, King Cyrus entered the city and was greeted by Daniel, now the ranking dignitary of the defeated Babylonians. Daniel showed him the portion of the scroll of Isaiah detailing his battle plan and written 200 years in advance. In the passage, God spoke of Cyrus by name and called him "My Anointed" who would permit the rebuilding of Jerusalem and the release of the Jewish people from their captivity. This so impressed Cyrus that he made Daniel part of his senior governing staff. And true to the prophecy, Cyrus released the Jews, returned the stolen Temple implements, and gave them permission to go back to Jerusalem and begin rebuilding their Temple.

Several decades earlier, Jeremiah had prophesied the Babylonian captivity would last 70 years, at the end of which Babylon would be defeated and the Jewish people would be free to return to Zion (**Jeremiah 25:12 & 27:7**). Isaiah had told them who would do it and how, and Jeremiah had told them when it would happen. Both were right, for by the testimony of two witnesses a thing is established (**Deuteronomy 19:15**).

Now you know the adult version.

CHAPTER TWENTY-SEVEN

DANIEL IN THE LION'S DEN

HOW DID DANIEL MAKE IT THROUGH THE NIGHT?

As we learned in the previous chapter, after about 70 years of absolute dominance over the known world, Babylon (Iraq) was conquered by a coalition of Persia (Iran) and Media (the Kurds) in about 538 BC. Thus began the rule of the Medo-Persian Empire, which lasted for 200 years or so until Alexander the Great conquered them.

THE BELOVED PROPHET

Daniel had enjoyed God's favor all his life. Darius, the new King of Persia and son-in-law of Cyrus, appointed Daniel as one of three administrators to oversee the kingdom. Daniel so distinguished himself that Darius gave him sole administrative authority over all the kingdom. This, of course, made the others jealous, and they sought to discredit him. But Daniel was trustworthy and neither corrupt nor negligent (**Daniel 6:4**). Finally, they devised a scheme to trap Daniel by making it illegal for him to worship God. They convinced Darius to make it mandatory for all his subjects to worship him for the next 30 days. Anyone caught worshipping anyone else must be thrown into a den of hungry lions (**Daniel 6:6-9**).

Daniel remained faithful to his God, and since he made no attempt to hide this, he was caught praying to Him a few days later. When Darius was told, he was greatly distressed because he liked Daniel and made every effort to save him. But even he had to obey the law, and so at sundown, Darius was forced to give the order to have Daniel arrested. As he watched Daniel being lowered into the lion's den he said to him, "Your God whom you serve continually, He will deliver you." Then he sealed up the den, went home and, refusing to eat or be entertained, spent a sleepless night alone (**Daniel 6:16-18**).

At dawn's first light, Darius hurried back to the lions' den and called out to Daniel "Has your God whom you serve continually been able to save you?" Daniel answered. "O King, live forever. My God sent His angel, and he shut the lions' mouths. They have not hurt me because I was found innocent in His sight. Nor have I done anything wrong before you, O King." (**Daniel 6:19-22**) Darius was overjoyed and gave the order to have Daniel lifted out of the lions' den. There was no wound or scratch on him because he had trusted God. Darius then had the men who had accused Daniel rounded up and thrown into the lions' den along with their wives and children. Before they reached the floor of the den, the lions overpowered them and crushed all their bones (**Daniel 6:23-24**).

TESTIMONY TIME

 Then King Darius wrote to all the nations and peoples of every language in all the earth:

"May you prosper greatly. I issue a decree that in every part of my kingdom people must fear and reverence the God of Daniel.

For He is the living God and He endures forever.

His Kingdom will not be destroyed; His dominion will never end.

He rescues and He saves, He performs signs and wonders in the heavens and on the Earth.

He has rescued Daniel from the power of the lions."

So Daniel prospered during the reign of Darius and the reign of Cyrus King of Persia (**Daniel 6:25-28**).

WHAT DO YOU MAKE OF THAT?

I think several important conclusions can be drawn:

1. From the original language of **Daniel 6:16-20** it appears that Darius believed God was obligated to save Daniel—because of the covenant that existed between them—and that He was able to do so. Darius was anxious to see if God would be as faithful to the covenant as Daniel had been. I believe he had the lion's' den sealed to keep the matter between Daniel and God—preventing Daniel's accusers from manipulating the outcome.

2. From his decree, you could conclude that God's faithfulness to Daniel converted Darius. And it prompted him to tell the world about the power of the Living God to rescue those He loves and who have chosen Him (See **1 Thessalonians 1:9-10**). Knowing there's someone who's always faithful and true to His word is a powerful attraction to one who has been betrayed and abandoned—experiences I'm sure Darius suffered just as you and I have.

3. In **Daniel 6:23** the word translated **trusted** means *to trust contin-ually*. The fact that the lions immediately devoured Daniel's accusers in the morning proves they had been hungry all night long. The only time Daniel knew from experience that they wouldn't devour him was after he had been rescued. All through the dark night of captivity, his had been a moment-by-moment series of contrary-to

feelings choices to believe God's promises in spite of his circum-stances—to live by faith, not by sight (**2 Corinthians 5:7**). This faith became one of the great examples in "The Hall of Faith" (**Hebrews 11:33**).

4. There's no indication God had warned Daniel of these events in advance. But surely Daniel had read **2 Chronicles 16:9**: "For the eyes of the Lord run to and fro throughout the whole Earth to show Himself strong on behalf of those whose heart is perfect toward Him." While we're cautioned not to put the Lord our God to the test (**Deuteronomy 6:16**), we also know that He who watches over Israel neither slumbers nor sleeps (**Psalm 121:4**), and we can do all things through Him who strengthens us (**Philippians 4:13**). Our victories over the enemy become powerful tools for evangelism.

5. Daniel's night in the Lion's den portrays our life on Earth. We're confined to this place and "our enemy the devil prowls around like a roaring lion looking for someone to devour" (**1 Peter 5:8**). But through faith, we're shielded by God's power until the coming of (our) salvation that is ready to be revealed in the last time (**1 Peter. 1:5**). Meanwhile, our King knows that God is obligated to save us, because of the covenant that exists between us, and that He is able to do so (**Romans 8:38-39**). He will declare God's name to His brothers and in the congregation He will praise Him (**Psalm 22:22**).

Now you know the adult version.

CHAPTER TWENTY-EIGHT

JONAH AND THE WHALE

WAS JONAH RESURRECTED FROM THE DEAD?

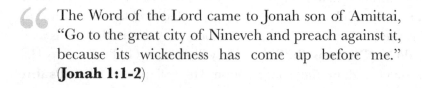

> The Word of the Lord came to Jonah son of Amittai, "Go to the great city of Nineveh and preach against it, because its wickedness has come up before me." (**Jonah 1:1-2**)

Jonah's name translates into English as *dove* and his father's name as *truth*, and **Nineveh** means *progeny*, so right away the story is intriguing to those of us who lean toward the mystical view. A dove showed Noah that God's judgment upon Earth had truly ended and the floodwaters were receding (**Genesis 8:11**). Peace had been restored between the Creator and His creation. For the poor, a dove was the prescribed offering for sin, restoring peace between the sinner and God (**Leviticus 5:7**). The Spirit of the Lord descended upon Jesus "like a dove" in **Matthew 3:16** and we know that He came to restore peace between mankind and God (**Colossians 1:19-20**). The story of Jonah involves restoring peace between the people of Nineveh and God and so it's fitting that He sent Dove, the offspring of Truth to warn His progeny.

But Jonah ran away from the Lord and headed for Tarshish (**Jonah 1:3**). Nineveh and Tarshish were at opposite ends of the known world. Nineveh was a great and wicked Gentile city on the banks of the Tigris River in what's now Eastern Iraq. And Tarshish was either modern Spain or England depending on which commentator you read. I lean toward England since the Phoenicians traded extensively there and their name for the place roughly translates into Britannia. (This view also makes more sense to me in interpreting **Ezekiel 38:13**.)

But, suffice it to say, God told Jonah to head east (Jonah came from the Galilee, **2 Kings 14:25**) and he booked passage on a boat heading west. By the way, this little tidbit shows us how little the religious leaders of Jesus' day knew about the history of their prophets. In attempting to prove that Jesus couldn't be a prophet, they said, "A prophet does not come out of Galilee" (**John 7:25**) when in fact both Jonah and Nahum came from there. (The name of Peter's hometown **Capernaum** means *village of Nahum*.)

THE PERFECT STORM

On the way to Tarshish, the voyagers encountered a terrible storm, so bad it threatened to capsize the boat. Believing the storm to be sent from God, the sailors finally determined that Jonah was the reason for it, so Jonah asked them to throw him overboard. As soon as they did, the storm subsided, and God sent a great fish that swallowed Jonah and kept him inside for 3 days and 3 nights (**Jonah 1:4-17**).

If you read chapter two literally and consult the original language, you'll have to conclude that Jonah died and while his body remained inside the whale, his spirit went to Sheol, the abode of the dead. **Sheol** is a Hebrew word translated *Hades* in Greek, or *Hell* in English. Before the cross it was the place where everyone went upon dying because Jesus had not yet settled the sin problem once and for all.

Sheol was separated by a vast chasm into two areas, a place of comfort for the faithful and a place of torment for those who had rejected God. The place of comfort was popularly called Paradise, or Abraham's bosom (**Luke 16:22-26**). When Jesus died, He went there and took the one crucified with Him who had asked Him to "Remember me when You come into Your Kingdom." (**Luke 23:42-43**)

When He rose from the grave, He took the faithful dead with Him into Heaven (**Matthew 27:53**) since His shed blood had finally erased the sins their sacrifices had only temporarily set aside. Since then, all who die in faith go directly to be with the Lord (**Philippians 1:22-23**).

COULD I TRY THIS AGAIN?

While in Sheol, Jonah asked for and received another chance to be faithful. The end of his prayer is remarkable in that it speaks of the Grace of God and declares the name of Jesus. (**Yeshua**, translated *Salvation comes from the Lord* in **Jonah 2:8-9**.)

When the whale spit the resurrected Jonah onto dry ground, he went to Nineveh. He began to preach, and was both astonished and angered when, from the king on down, those wicked Gentiles immediately began to repent.

"I knew you would do this," he cried to God, "That's why I ran to Tarshish. I knew that You are a gracious and compassionate God, slow to anger and abounding in love." (**Jonah 4:1-2**) Then God caused a vine to grow and die as an object lesson to show Jonah that he was more concerned about the vine than about the people of Nineveh. After all, the vine brought him relief from the hot sun. What had the people of Nineveh done for him?

But remember, Nineveh means progeny. From God's point of view, we are all His children, Jew and Gentile, saint and sinner, and deserving of a chance to repent and live. When we respond favorably, all is immediately forgiven and forgotten.

THE SIGN OF THE PROPHET JONAH

When, for the umpteenth time, the Jews asked Jesus for a sign, He said no sign would be given except for the sign of the Prophet Jonah. "For as Jonah was three days and three nights in the belly of the huge fish, so the Son of Man will be three days and three nights in the belly of the Earth" (**Matthew 12:40**). This reference validates Jonah's role as a prophet in Israel, verifies the accuracy of his story and points to the Lord's own resurrection. But what's the deeper meaning to all this?

First, Jonah is like all of us. Seeking God's grace for our own deliverance, we desire only justice for our enemies and we are often angry when He shows them mercy. But the story of Jonah is also a parable of Israel and the Gentiles. Israel also failed in her first effort to fulfill her mission as God's witness (**Isaiah 43:10-13**) and ceased to exist as a nation. And just as in Jonah's failure, a boatload of sailors came to know the Lord and were saved (**Jonah 1:15-16**), so in Israel's failure a multitude of Gentiles have come to know the Lord and be saved.

But Jonah returned from the dead, and in his second attempt, the people of Nineveh repented and were spared from judgment to regain their lives. Israel has also returned from the dead. And in the remnant of Israel's faithfulness at the end of the age, more multitudes of God's progeny will repent and be spared from judgment to receive eternal life.

Now you know the adult version.

PART II

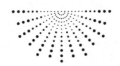

The New Testament

CHAPTER TWENTY-NINE

THE BIRTH OF JOHN THE BAPTIST

A SPECIAL PASSOVER GIFT

After years of faithful service, Zechariah of the tribe of Levi was now a senior priest in Israel, assigned to Temple work. Years earlier, he had married Elizabeth. And though they had prayed and prayed, and tried and tried, throughout their long life together they had been unable to have children.

That all changed on the day the Angel Gabriel visited Zechariah during one of his tours of duty (**Luke 1:8-11**). Zechariah was the priest chosen by lot that day to offer prayers at the Golden Altar that stands at the entrance to the Holy of Holies in the Temple. This was already a once in a lifetime honor but Gabriel's sudden appearance beside the altar, announcing that Zechariah and Elizabeth would soon have a son, made it totally unique. Only a few times before had something similar taken place, also involving barren women and foretelling great blessing for Israel, but never had anything like it happened in the Holy of Holies.

The most famous previous case was Abraham and Sarah, who were promised a son by the Lord Himself. But there were others, too. The Angel of the Lord visited the childless parents of Samson, announcing the son they would soon have would be a powerful man who would begin the deliverance of Israel from the Philistines (**Judges 13**). And, Hannah, after praying for years (and finally promising God she would give her son to the priests in the Tabernacle to be raised for service to Him), was given a son she named Samuel. He was the first of Israel's great prophets and at the Lord's direction anointed both Saul and David to be King (**1 Samuel 1**). Now, Zechariah was being told that his son would be the one to proclaim the coming Messiah and prepare the people to receive Him. And like Samson and Samuel before him, John was to be a lifelong Nazarite (see **Numbers 6:1-21**), set aside by a special vow for service to the Lord for as long as he lived.

WHAT DO YOU HAVE TO SAY ABOUT THAT?

Having been childless for so long, Zechariah was understandably skeptical and asked for some assurance that this would really happen. In response, Gabriel struck him dumb for doubting the words of God's messenger, rendering him speechless until the baby was born.

In those days, priests on duty stayed in rooms in the Temple, but as soon as his Temple duties were complete, he rushed home to Elizabeth. Gabriel had told Zechariah that his son would also minister to the people in the spirit and power of Elijah, so as he left he grabbed Elijah's mantle from the cabinet beneath the incense altar where it had been stored for many years. His son would have use for it.

Nine months later, on their son's eighth day of life, they took him to be circumcised according to the provisions of the Old Covenant. There, Zechariah spoke his first words since Gabriel's visit, confirming their baby would be named John, **Jochanin** in Hebrew, which means *favored of God*.

One of the fascinating things about John the Baptist is his relationship to Jesus. Mary and Elizabeth were related, and it was to Elizabeth that Mary went for comfort during the early days of her pregnancy. Luke writes that John jumped for joy in his mother's womb upon hearing Mary's voice when she was expecting Jesus (**Luke 1:41**). John and Jesus were only six months apart in age and most probably knew each other when they were young. In fact, the key to determining the timing of the Lord's birth is discovering when John was born, so let's find out.

First, we have to assume that wanting a son more than anything (it was a woman's crowning achievement in that era, whereas being barren was considered a punishment from God) Zechariah and Elizabeth went about the process of conception immediately upon his return home from his Temple rotation. So when was that?

CHOOSING TEAMS

Nearly 1,000 years earlier, King David had divided the priests into 24 courses (divisions) to serve rotating one-week periods in the temple. All 24 divisions served during all the Feasts, and each one also served a weeklong stint twice a year on a rotating schedule. The religious year began about mid-March on our calendar, and right away there were nearly three weeks of preparation and Feasts: Passover, the Feast of Unleavened Bread, and First Fruits. Then the divisions began their rotation.

Comparing **Luke 1:5** to **1 Chronicles 24:10** shows that Zechariah was of the division of Abijah, number eight in the weekly rotation. Counting the time all were on duty, and the eight weeks in rotation when Zechariah's turn came, puts the visit by Gabriel about three months into the religious year. Assuming Elizabeth became pregnant right away, a normal nine-month gestation period would place the birth of John the Baptist at the beginning of the following religious year (mid-March remember), and indeed there are many who believe he was born on Passover.

There is some speculation here, but not much, and so it's reasonable to assume that John's birth occurred in the spring. If that's so, then our Lord was born around the time of the Jewish New Year, Rosh Hashanah, six months later. As we'll see in the next chapter, that makes a lot of sense, too.

Now you know the adult version.

CHAPTER THIRTY

THE BIRTH OF JESUS

WHEN DOES LIFE BEGIN?

The story is all too familiar. Caesar Augustus had ordered that a census be taken of the entire Roman Empire, requiring everyone to register in the town of their family origin. Joseph and Mary, in the final days of her pregnancy, journeyed for several days from Nazareth to reach Bethlehem, the home of their ancestor, King David. 750 years earlier, the prophet Micah had foreseen this time and had written that the Messiah would be born there.

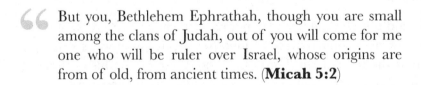

> But you, Bethlehem Ephrathah, though you are small among the clans of Judah, out of you will come for me one who will be ruler over Israel, whose origins are from of old, from ancient times. (**Micah 5:2**)

Finding no suitable accommodations because of the crowds, they finally settled into a manger where the Christ child was born. In a field outside of town, shepherds watching the Temple flocks were the first to learn that the long-awaited Messiah had come. The skies

opened up, and a Heavenly choir announced the best news anyone
has ever heard.

WHEN WERE YOU BORN?

Celebrating the Lord's birthday on December 25 is a tradition that's
probably only about 1,300 or 1,400 years old. "Wait a minute," you
say, "There's a 600-year gap. What did people do before then?"
Let's find out.

Many believe the December date came to be as a result of the inte-
gration of Christianity into the Roman Empire as first a permitted
belief and later the official religion of the Empire. Previously, it had
been outlawed and its practice punishable by death. But the
Emperor Constantine changed all that, and the worship of Jesus
was made legitimate. And in the fourth century, what would be the
Holy Roman Empire was born—with Christianity as the official
religion.

You know how deeply ingrained traditions become. For as long as
anyone could remember, the pagan Feast of Saturnalia had been a
part of Roman life, celebrated at the time of the winter solstice.
Rather than upset the tradition, or replace pagan practices with
Christian ones, this feast was declared to be the day of our Lord's
birth. Knowing its origin, many Christians did not accept this date
and for several hundred years refused to celebrate it as such. Hence
the gap.

To find out His real birthday requires some detective work, and the
biggest clues come to us from John the Baptist. John was six months
old at the time of the Lord's birth, and discovering his birthday is
somewhat easier. So in the previous chapter, we started there.

Our conclusion was that the birth of John the Baptist occurred at
the beginning of the religious year (mid-March, remember) and
indeed many believe he was born on Passover.

Let's convert this to our calendar to avoid further confusion and discover a fascinating possibility about December 25th in the process. In all probability, John the Baptist was conceived in mid-June and born the following March.

According to **Luke 1:26-27** Mary conceived in the sixth month of Elizabeth's pregnancy. That means our Lord was conceived in late December and born in September. Are we inadvertently celebrating His conception at Christmas instead of His birth? And was Heaven making a statement to Earth concerning the origin of life?

SEPTEMBER SONG

Among Messianic Jews, there are two primary schools of thought concerning the September birth. Both have valid points, and both are based on the notion that the Jewish Feasts have both historical and prophetic significance.

The first school of thought places the Lord's birth at the Feast of Tabernacles, since that feast commemorates the time of the Lord's dwelling with His people.

The second places the Lord's birth on Rosh Hashanah, because according to Jewish tradition, both the Earth (as we know it) and Adam were born on that day and the Lord is the "Last Adam" (**1 Corinthians 15:45**).

For this reason, as well as the prevalence of trumpets in its celebration, (it's also called The Feast of Trumpets, and trumpets always accompanied the birth of a King's son) I personally prefer Rosh Hashanah. I believe the Second Coming will also take place on this day. But regardless of which date you prefer, from all that the Bible, Jewish tradition, and Church history tell us, September is the time to sing "Happy Birthday, Lord Jesus."

Other factors favor a fall birth as well. We know there were shepherds tending sheep in the fields outside Bethlehem on the night of the Lord's birth. That means they were living in the open fields with the sheep (**Luke 2:8**). Winter weather doesn't permit this practice much past late fall in that region. Also, it's highly unlikely the Roman Governor would call for a census, requiring everyone to be uprooted to travel to their ancestral homes, camping outside along the way in the dead of winter.

By the way, Israel's weather can be confusing since in the North communities around the Sea of Galilee are often warm even in winter while Jerusalem in the south can actually get snowed on from time to time. That's because the weather there is more a function of the altitude than the latitude. The Sea of Galilee is 600 feet below sea level making it warmer than you'd expect whereas Jerusalem is about 3,700 feet above. Then within 50 miles to the East from Jerusalem, you drop over 5,000 feet to the Dead Sea where it's a desert climate year round.

THE LIGHT OF THE WORLD

Mary's statement upon learning that she had become pregnant, "I am the Lord's servant. May it be done to me as you have said," is from a prayer traditionally offered at Hanukkah. As I said earlier, if He was born in September, He would have been conceived the previous December. Was the "Light of the World" conceived during the Festival of Lights?

If so, Christmas really began at the moment of divine conception. God the Father planned it, God the Holy Spirit planted the fertilized seed in Mary, and at that moment God the Son took on human form—the form of an embryo, a fetus in the womb of a virgin. From that first moment of conception Jesus was fully alive, fully human, and fully God. He didn't become the Incarnate God somewhere along the path of His life, or even when He emerged from Mary's womb. He had been, from the moment of conception (**Luke 1:35**). God could not have made any stronger statement about the sanctity of pre-born life.

By the way, as a poor, unwed teenaged girl about to be ostracized from family and society, Mary met all the modern criteria for an abortion. Had she and Joseph sought one, it would have been just as much the murder of the Messiah as was His death on the cross some 30 years later. So the life of the Christ child really did begin at Christmas.

BUT WAIT THERE'S MORE

Here are a couple of other tidbits to add to your knowledge of this unique event. Typically a father hired musicians to stand by as the time of a first child's birth drew near. If the child was a son, the musicians went through the community, playing and singing the good news. Since Mary and Joseph were a long way from home and too poor to afford musicians, the Lord's real Father in Heaven provided His own musicians. The angelic choir filled the skies to proclaim the special event.

The sheep being tended in the fields outside Bethlehem that night belonged to the Temple. They were bred especially for sale to visiting pilgrims as sacrificial lambs for their sin offerings. In other words, they were born to die for the sins of the people. How fitting that the shepherds tending those sheep were the first to see The Lamb born to die for the sins of the people.

The priests who worked in the Temple wore linen undergarments to protect their modesty. When the undergarments wore out, they were cut into strips and braided together to form the wicks used in the giant menorah placed in the Temple courtyard during Hanukkah. These garments were called swaddling cloths, and when they were immersed in oil and set afire, their light illuminated the whole city. When Jesus was born, Mary wrapped Him in swaddling cloths and later, when immersed in the power of the Holy Spirit, His Light illuminated the whole world.

The Lamb was born to die for the sins of the people, the Light of the World had come, and the world would never be the same again.

Now you know the adult version.

CHAPTER THIRTY-ONE

WE THREE KINGS OF ORIENT ARE

THERE WEREN'T THREE, AND THEY WEREN'T KINGS

> After Jesus was born in Bethlehem in Judea during the time of King Herod, Magi came from the east to Jerusalem and asked "Where is the one who has been born king of the Jews? We saw his star in the east and have come to worship him." (**Matthew 2:1-2**)

LET'S BEGIN AT THE BEGINNING

This story actually began just over 600 years earlier during the life of Daniel the Prophet. As you know from chapter 25, as a teenager, Daniel, a prince of Israel, was taken hostage by the King of Babylon to ensure that the peace treaty between Israel and Babylon would be obeyed. But Israel's kings repeatedly violated the treaty, and so the Babylonians burned Jerusalem and Solomon's Temple to the ground and took all the Jews captive to Babylon where they remained for 70 years. Toward the end of this 70 Year period, Daniel, now an old man, was praying to God, asking for the release of His people. While praying, he was visited by the Angel Gabriel and given a message that has become the single most important piece of prophetic Scripture in the entire Bible. This message is contained in **Daniel 9:24-27** and revealed the time of the Messiah's coming, His subsequent death and the destruction of Jerusalem, and an overview of the events leading up to the End of the Age.

Daniel had become the head of a group of royal advisors who were both wise and spiritual. According to tradition, he shared Gabriel's message with them and admonished them to incorporate it into their wisdom, to be handed down from generation to generation until the time of the Messiah's birth. Over the following 500 years, this group became a powerful priesthood that was so influential in the affairs of the kingdom (now called Parthia) that no king could reign without their approval. Central to their philosophy was the belief handed down to them over the centuries that one day soon, God would send One who would be born to the throne putting to an end all the intrigue that usually accompanied the appointment of a king. The general time of the coming of this King was known to them from Daniel's teaching, as was the sign they would be given. A special star would appear in the sky, marking His arrival (**Numbers 24:17**).

THE SIGN OF THE STAR

When the star appeared, a delegation of this Parthian priesthood, known as Magi, set out for Jerusalem. There were undoubtedly more than three of them since dignitaries of the day traveled in a great entourage both for protection and as a sign of their importance. In this case, they were also traveling through enemy territory, since a few years earlier Parthia had repelled a Roman invasion and the Romans were now entrenched in Israel. No wonder Herod—and indeed all Jerusalem—were disturbed by their arrival (**Matthew 2:3**). Keep in mind, Herod was not even Jewish. He was an Idumean (Jordanian) who had been appointed by the Romans, and now powerful foreign kingmakers were coming to claim that there was one who was born to be King of the Jews. Surely this natural-born king would have a more powerful claim to the throne than a foreign appointee. Imagine Herod's fear when they came asking, "Where is the one who has been born King of the Jews?"

WILL THE REAL KING PLEASE STAND UP?

When Herod summoned the Jewish scholars for information regarding this king, they concluded from **Micah 5:2** that the Messiah would come from Bethlehem. Herod then met secretly with the Magi and determined the time when the star had first appeared. He sent them to Bethlehem in search of the child, hoping to learn through them of His whereabouts (**Matthew 2:4-8**).

Guided by the star, the Magi came to the house where Jesus and Mary and Joseph were now staying. They presented Him with three gifts rich in symbolism and worshiped Him there. The gold they gave Him signified royalty and identified Him as a King, the frankincense spoke of His Priesthood, and the myrrh was a prophecy of His death since myrrh was known primarily as an embalming spice. These three gifts represented the three offices of the Messiah: King, Priest and Prophet. (In the millennium, the Messiah will once again be given gifts, but this time only two: gold and frankincense. [**Isaiah 60:6**] No more death.)

The Magi, being warned in a dream, did not reveal the child's location to Herod and returned home by a different route (**Matthew 2:9-12**). When Herod realized this, he was furious and gave orders to kill all the boys in Bethlehem who were two years old and younger in accordance with the time he had learned from the Magi. But Joseph had been warned of Herod's anger and took his family into Egypt, remaining there until Herod died (**Matthew 2:13-16**).

From all of this, we can conclude that the Magi didn't arrive in Bethlehem on the night Jesus was born. They probably set out on their journey when the star first appeared, indicating the Lord's birth. Allowing time to confirm the sign of the star, make preparations to leave, and then travel nearly 800 miles, they could have arrived in Jerusalem as much as a year or two later. Hence the execution of all the boys in Bethlehem two years of age and younger.

LISTEN TO WHAT ISN'T SAID

Sometimes what isn't said in Scripture is as revealing as what is. Even after reading the prophecy in **Micah 5:2** and receiving the dual confirmation of the star and the arrival of the Magi, neither Herod nor the Jewish spiritual and political leaders went to Bethlehem themselves. We can understand Herod's response; he wasn't even Jewish and feared the discovery of a rival claim to the throne. But Israel had waited centuries for the Messiah, and these leaders had the same knowledge as the Magi. The prophecies were written in their own Scriptures and were being fulfilled right before their eyes. The problem was that the Jewish leadership had long before departed from a literal interpretation of Scripture, and the ruling Sadducean party had rejected predictive prophecy as unreliable and not meant for their time. Having deemed it irrelevant, they ignored it and missed the event they had longed for.

The spiritual and political leaders of our generation have made the same mistake, also denying the authority of predictive prophecy. Only this time it's for keeps. There's no prophecy of a Third Coming, so if they miss the signs of the Second Coming they will have missed their final chance. Once again it's proven true—the only thing we learn from history is that we learn nothing from history.

Now you know the adult version.

CHAPTER THIRTY-TWO

THE TEMPTATION IN THE WILDERNESS

A SUREFIRE WAY TO BEAT THE DEVIL

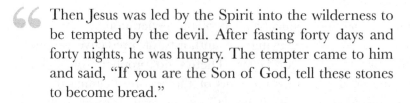

> Then Jesus was led by the Spirit into the wilderness to be tempted by the devil. After fasting forty days and forty nights, he was hungry. The tempter came to him and said, "If you are the Son of God, tell these stones to become bread."
>
> Jesus answered, "It is written: 'Man does not live on bread alone, but on every word that comes from the mouth of God.'"
>
> Then the devil took him to the holy city and had him stand on the highest point of the temple. "If you are the Son of God," he said, "throw yourself down. For it is written: 'He will command his angels concerning you, and they will lift you up in their hands, so that you will not strike your foot against a stone.'" Jesus answered him, "It is also written: 'Do not put the Lord your God to the test.'" Again, the devil took him to a

very high mountain and showed him all the kingdoms of the world and their splendor. "All this I will give you," he said, "if you will bow down and worship me."

Jesus said to him, "Away from me, Satan! For it is written: 'Worship the Lord your God, and serve him only.'" Then the devil left him, and angels came and attended him. (**Matthew 4:1-11**)

This event took place just after the Lord's baptism when the Spirit of God descended like a dove to rest upon Him. This visible sign of the Spirit was a special anointing to confirm His ministry to John, and to equip Jesus for His work as our Messiah.

THE NUMBER OF TESTING

The 40-day fast is also a special act of consecration. Moses (**Exodus 24:18**) and Elijah (**1 Kings 19:8**) underwent similar preparation and the emerging Nation of Israel endured 40 years of testing (**Exodus 16:4**). Forty is known as the number of testing from these events.

There is an excellent model for spiritual warfare to be found here. The Lord never disputed the devil, but always answered him with Scripture. If you're going up against the enemy, your best weapon is the double-edged sword (**Hebrews 4:12**). But you better know what you're talking about, because the devil can quote Scripture too, as we see here.

And by the nature of the temptations, you can see that the devil didn't doubt the power of God. No, that wasn't the issue, but rather if Jesus would remain obedient to His mission. You see, in order for things to work out successfully for us, Jesus had to set aside His incredible power to live the life of a man, and exercise only those abilities common to us.

He didn't come as an angel to redeem angels, nor as a King to just redeem kings, but as a man, and the lowliest of us at that, to redeem mankind. He voluntarily stepped down off the Throne of the Universe to become the humblest of men. He had no beauty or majesty to attract us to him, nothing in his appearance that we should desire him (**Isaiah 53:2**). All His miracles were performed in the power of the Holy Spirit, and that's the reason He could say to His disciples, "I tell you the truth, anyone who has faith in me will do what I have been doing. He will do even greater things than these, because I am going to the Father." (**John 14:12**)

I don't know if you can comprehend what a come down that is. I know I can't. "What is man that you are mindful of him, the son of man that you care for him?" says David in **Psalm 8:4**. How would you compare the value of God to the value of man? What species can you look down to as a human to approximate the distance from God to you? A bug? Would you agree to become a bug forever to save bugs from their sins? And then hold firm to your commitment after a 40-day fast while being promised all the treasure of the universe? Think about it!

It's especially important to note that Jesus didn't dispute the devil's claim to ownership of the Kingdoms of the world. As the Apostle John would later write, "We know that we are children of God and that the whole world is under the control of the evil one." (**1 John 5:19**)

Those who blame God when things go wrong simply don't understand that. Satan stole the world from Adam, and at the cross Jesus ransomed it back. While during this age, Satan still exercises power here. One day soon the Lord will return and lay claim to that for which He's paid, and that old usurper the devil will finally get his due.

 Then the devil left him, and angels came and attended him. (**Matthew 4:11**)

Now you know the adult version.

CHAPTER THIRTY-THREE

JESUS HEALS A PARALYTIC

DESPERATE ACTS TO GET TO JESUS

" A few days later, when Jesus again entered Capernaum, the people heard that he had come home. They gathered in such large numbers that there was no room left, not even outside the door, and he preached the word to them. Some men came, bringing to him a paralyzed man, carried by four of them. Since they could not get him to Jesus because of the crowd, they made an opening in the roof above Jesus by digging through it and then lowered the mat the man was lying on. When Jesus saw their faith, he said to the paralyzed man, "Son, your sins are forgiven."

Now some teachers of the law were sitting there, thinking to themselves, "Why does this fellow talk like that? He's blaspheming! Who can forgive sins but God alone?"

Immediately Jesus knew in his spirit that this was what
they were thinking in their hearts, and he said to them,
"Why are you thinking these things? Which is easier: to
say to the paralyzed man, 'Your sins are forgiven,' or to
say, 'Get up, take your mat and walk'? But I want you
to know that the Son of Man has authority on earth to
forgive sins." So he said to the man, "I tell you, get up,
take your mat and go home." He got up, took his mat
and walked out in full view of them all. This amazed
everyone and they praised God, saying, "We have
never seen anything like this!" (**Mark 2:1-12**)

WHERE DO YOU COME FROM?

Home, for Jesus, meant back to the Galilee village of Capernaum. It
was really His adopted hometown, the place where Peter lived. He
and the disciples had been in the neighboring villages, preaching
and healing the sick. Ever since He had cast out an evil spirit in the
synagogue, and then healed Peter's mother-in-law, the crowds
followed Him everywhere.

And so, it wasn't long before a large crowd had gathered outside
Peter's house again. Unable to get close to Jesus, a group of men
had chopped a hole in Peter's roof and lowered their paralyzed
friend through the hole to where Jesus stood.

The Teachers of the Law were correct in stating that only God can
forgive sins, but missed the comparison Jesus made for them. Saying,
"Son, your sins are forgiven," is an easy thing to do and who can tell
if you're legitimate or not? There's no visible evidence. So to prove
He had the authority to forgive sins, Jesus commanded the paralyzed man to get up, pick up his mat and go home.

As the man obeyed, his visible healing was evident to all and
presented indisputable proof that Jesus is Who He claimed to be.
The man's sins were forgiven and his paralyzed limbs made whole.
The One Who had done this looked like a man, and He was. But by
exercising authority only God possesses, He had proved to one and

all that He was also God. In the flesh. The people were right in saying, "We have never seen anything like this!" Nothing like this had ever happened. Heaven had invaded Earth, and nothing would ever be the same again.

Now you know the adult version.

CHAPTER THIRTY-FOUR

WATER INTO WINE

A FAVOR THAT DEFINED A MINISTRY

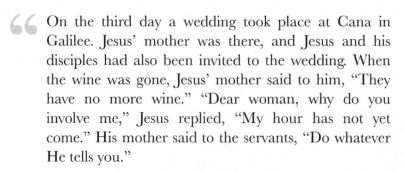

On the third day a wedding took place at Cana in Galilee. Jesus' mother was there, and Jesus and his disciples had also been invited to the wedding. When the wine was gone, Jesus' mother said to him, "They have no more wine." "Dear woman, why do you involve me," Jesus replied, "My hour has not yet come." His mother said to the servants, "Do whatever He tells you."

Nearby stood six stone water jars, the kind the Jews use for ceremonial washing, each holding from 20 to 30 gallons. Jesus said to the servants, "Fill the jars with water," so they filled them to the brim. Then he said to them, "Now draw some out and take it to the master of the banquet."

They did so, and the master of the banquet tasted the water that had been turned into wine. He did not realize where it had come from although the servants who had drawn the water knew. Then he called the bridegroom aside and said, "Everyone brings out the choice wine first and then the cheaper wine after the guests have had too much to drink, but you have saved the best till now."

This, the first of his miraculous signs, Jesus performed in Cana of Galilee. He thus revealed his glory and the disciples put their faith in him. (**John 2:1-11**)

WHAT WAS THAT AGAIN?

Aside from the fact that changing water into wine requires supernatural ability, the most astonishing thing about this miracle is that because of it "He thus revealed His Glory and the disciples put their faith in Him." Helping a friend with a beverage problem as a favor to His mom? Many commentators put this miracle way down their list of great things Jesus did—if they include it at all. But John put it first and attached considerable significance to it. Must be more going on here than meets the eye.

By the way, a couple of interesting bits of trivia will help in our understanding. The third day of the week is Tuesday on the Jewish calendar and is still the preferred day for weddings in Israel. That's because on the original third day, God pronounced things *good* twice —the only time He did so in the six days of Creation. Therefore, the third day is known as a day of double blessing, the best day of the week to begin a new life together. Also, Jewish wedding feasts lasted for seven days, and to run out of wine so early would have been embarrassing to say the least. That's probably why Mary asked Jesus to get involved in something that was really not their concern.

And lastly, the stone jars held water normally used only for ceremonial washing, a symbolic act of cleansing from sin, not for cleaning off the dust of the road or other dirt. They were placed at the door so a person would not enter a friend's house in a ceremonially "unclean" state and contaminate the house. By dipping their fingers into the water and wiping them dry, a person would symbolically "wash away their sins" and be ceremonially clean. When we say, "I'm washing my hands of this matter," we really mean we're trying to absolve ourselves of any responsibility for it. The phrase comes from this practice, which was soon to be immortalized by Pontius Pilate during Jesus' trial and conviction. Some believe that this water would also have contained a sprinkling of ashes from a red heifer, in case anyone had inadvertently touched something dead (see **Numbers 19**).

LET'S GET MYSTICAL

John was a mystic. His Gospel is highly symbolic in the way it presents facts about the Lord and His ministry. He made no attempt to portray events in their chronological order, chose only seven miracles, followed by seven discourses and seven "I am" statements:

I am the Bread of Life, **John 6:35**

I am the Light of the World, **John 8:12**

I am the Gate, **John 10:7**

I am the Good Shepherd, **John 10:11**

I am the Resurrection and the Life, **John 11:25**

I am the Way, the Truth, and the Life, **John 14:6**

I am the Vine, **John 15:1**

His entire Gospel covers only about 21 days out of three and a half years of the Lord's ministry, devotes 10 chapters to just one week, and over one quarter (237 of 879 verses) describe just one day. The richness of John's symbolism makes his Gospel a favorite among those who view Scripture from a high level of inspiration, and his story of the wedding at Cana is the crowning touch. Let's look at it through his eyes.

Jesus commanded unnamed servants to completely fill six (the number of man) jars that were stone, cold, and empty (a model of our unregenerate hearts, **Ezekiel 36:25-27**) with water. In **John 16:5-14** the Holy Spirit is described as One who would not speak of Himself, but only of Jesus. In fact, the only name by which we know the Holy Spirit is actually His job description, Comforter (KJV) or Counselor (NIV). This title is derived from the Greek word **parakletos**, which can also be translated *intercessor* or *advocate*. These servants are a model of the Holy Spirit, Who accomplishes the work of regeneration in our hearts (**Titus 3:4-7**), filling us with Living Water (**John 7:37-39**).

The water, normally used for ceremonial cleansing, immediately turned to wine and so that which had only temporarily cleansed a person from sin now became symbolic of the Blood of Jesus that washes us clean forever (**Luke 22:20**). The master of the banquet remarked that the bridegroom had saved the best till last, signifying that the New Covenant that permanently cleanses us (represented by the wine), is far superior to the Old Covenant that only temporarily set aside our sins (represented by the water and ashes). Thus by this miracle, Jesus truly did reveal His Glory, and you can see why the disciples put their faith in Him.

Now you know the adult version.

CHAPTER THIRTY-FIVE

JESUS HEALS A DEMON POSSESSED MAN

THE CASE OF THE DEVILED HAM

> They went across the lake to the region of the Gerasenes (Gadarenes). When Jesus got out of the boat, a man with an evil spirit came from the tombs to meet him. This man lived in the tombs, and no one could bind him anymore, not even with a chain. For he had often been chained hand and foot, but he tore the chains apart and broke the irons on his feet. No one was strong enough to subdue him. Night and day among the tombs and in the hills he would cry out and cut himself with stones.
>
> When he saw Jesus from a distance, he ran and fell on his knees in front of him. He shouted at the top of his voice, "What do you want with me, Jesus, Son of the Most High God? Swear to God that you won't torture me!" For Jesus had said to him, "Come out of this man, you evil spirit!" Then Jesus asked him, "What is your name?" "My name is Legion," he replied, "for we

are many." And he begged Jesus again and again not to send them out of the area.

A large herd of pigs was feeding on the nearby hillside. The demons begged Jesus, "Send us among the pigs; allow us to go into them." He gave them permission, and the evil spirits came out and went into the pigs. The herd, about two thousand in number, rushed down the steep bank into the lake and were drowned.

Those tending the pigs ran off and reported this in the town and countryside, and the people went out to see what had happened. When they came to Jesus, they saw the man who had been possessed by the legion of demons, sitting there, dressed and in his right mind; and they were afraid. Those who had seen it told the people what had happened to the demon-possessed man—and told about the pigs as well. Then the people began to plead with Jesus to leave their region.

As Jesus was getting into the boat, the man who had been demon-possessed begged to go with him. Jesus did not let him, but said, "Go home to your own people and tell them how much the Lord has done for you, and how he has had mercy on you." So the man went away and began to tell in the Decapolis how much Jesus had done for him. And all the people were amazed. (**Mark 5:1-20**)

Two details of this story tell us we're in Gentile country. The most obvious, a herd of 2,000 pigs for which there would be no market among the Jews. And second, the healed man went throughout the Decapolis to make it clear. The Decapolis (literally ten cities) was a Gentile area East of the Sea of Galilee in what's mostly Jordan today. These ten cities were all free, and had joined together in a loose confederacy for economic and military benefit. Perhaps the possessed man was from Gadara, known today as Umm Qais, one of the area's major cities. Gadara commanded magnificent views over the northern Jordan Valley, the Sea of Galilee, the Yarmouk River gorge and the Golan Heights, and was not far from Capernaum.

There are some interesting opinions about the nature of demons. They're not the devil but have agreed to serve him. Some believe they're the disembodied spirits of the angels who rebelled with Satan and co-mingled with human females before the Flood. They desire two things, worship, standing behind the otherwise impotent pagan gods (**1 Corinthians 10:20**), and physical embodiment. In fact, they begged Jesus to let them inhabit a herd of pigs rather than join their compatriots in the prison of the abyss (**Jude 6**). At the end of the age, doctrines taught by demons will deceive those people without the protective power of the Spirit of God (**1 Timothy 4:1**) in Satan's final attempt to deceive mankind. Many see the strange creatures John called locusts and other supernatural warriors of Revelation as being demonic.

WHAT HAS COME OVER YOU?

Born again Christians cannot be demon possessed, but many believers are oppressed and harassed by them. Our unconfessed sins place us temporarily out of fellowship with God, and make us fair game for the enemy's schemes. **1 Peter 5:8** tells us to be sober-minded and alert because the devil prowls around like a roaring lion, seeking someone to devour. **2 Corinthians 2:11** tells us to forgive so that Satan won't outwit us.

Until a few centuries ago, demon possession was commonly held to be the cause of all manner of sickness and disease, and casting them out with prayer was a prescribed remedy. Today, the medical profession treats these kinds of maladies with narcotics and laughs at anyone's suggestion that they might be caused by the demonic.

It is clear from this passage in Mark that the Lord has absolute authority over the demons. And in most appearances they make in Scripture, you'll find them disclosing His true identity showing the truth of **James 2:19**—The demons believe, and tremble. Whenever that happened, the Lord immediately silenced them, not desiring that kind of testimony.

PRISONS OF OUR OWN MAKING

Most unbelievers today deny the existence of demons. The superstitious Gentiles of the Lord's day were the opposite. They attributed great power to these demons and were afraid of the Lord when He showed Himself to be superior to them. Not wanting to find themselves in the middle of a big spiritual battle, and concerned about the loss of revenue due to the drowned pigs, they begged Him to leave. And so He did.

Jesus still sets people free. He sent His Holy Spirit to dwell in us at the moment we believed. His power is in us to drive out demons (**Matthew 10:8**).

Now you know the adult version.

CHAPTER THIRTY-SIX

JESUS HEALS A LEPER

A MODEL OF SINS FORGIVEN

> While Jesus was in one of the towns, a man came along who was covered with leprosy. When he saw Jesus, he fell with his face to the ground and begged him, "Lord, if you are willing, you can make me clean." Jesus reached out his hand and touched the man. "I am willing," he said. "Be clean!" And immediately the leprosy left him. (**Luke 5:12-13**)

Throughout the Bible, leprosy is given a special significance. From earliest times, it was seen as a punishment for sins, since it eats the body away physically like sin can eat at us emotionally. Leprosy was the dreaded disease of the day, because there was no cure and contracting the disease sentenced one to a life of loneliness and poverty as well as pain. Lepers were quarantined—kept separate from the rest of the community and even from family and friends. They couldn't work to support themselves and their families since they were confined to colonies populated by others like themselves.

When a leper came near another person, he had to shout in a loud voice, "Unclean. Unclean." What a blow to their self-esteem.

Leprosy is called Hansen's disease today, and (as of 2017) the World Health Organization has treated 16 million people with leprosy over the past 20 years. The Lord used a case of leprosy to validate to Moses that He is Who He claims to be, in the Bible's first mention of the disease, when He called Moses to set the Israelites free from slavery in Egypt.

 Then the LORD said, "Put your hand inside your cloak." So Moses put his hand into his cloak, and when he took it out, it was leprous, like snow. "Now put it back into your cloak," he said. So Moses put his hand back into his cloak, and when he took it out, it was restored, like the rest of his flesh. (**Exodus 4:6-7**)

THE PRINCIPLE OF FIRST MENTION

The first appearance of a word in the Bible is usually significant. The first mention of blood, for instance, occurs in **Genesis 4** in conjunction with Cain's murder of Abel. The passage conveys the idea that the essence of life is contained in the blood. Later the eating or drinking of blood was forbidden.

The first mention of leprosy demonstrates the Lord's authority over the disease, something no man could claim. Contracting and then being cured of this frightening disease convinced Moses he was in the very presence of God.

No miraculous healing carried greater significance in Biblical Israel than the cleansing of a leper—because the disease was thought to be a punishment for sins. Curing it was tantamount to forgiving sins, and anytime someone was healed, he or she had to go to the priest to have the healing confirmed and the proper offerings of thanksgiving presented to God. Needless to say, this didn't happen often, so when Jesus began healing lepers, the word spread like wildfire.

The unnamed leper in our passage above became convinced that Jesus could heal him, perhaps because of the great number of healings the Lord was performing. The sheer number of healings had the whole countryside abuzz.

I love the phrase, "Lord, if you're willing," that the leper used in asking for healing. It says he was convinced of the Lord's ability and was only uncertain about His desire. I haven't found a single instance in Scripture where the Lord was unwilling to respond to anyone anywhere who asked in faith. His response is always like the one He gave to the leper. "I am willing."

Now you know the adult version.

CHAPTER THIRTY-SEVEN

THE KINGDOM PARABLES

ISRAEL, THE CHURCH, AND THE KINGDOM

The Kingdom Parables are found in **Matthew 13**. In the previous chapter of Matthew, the Jewish leadership had attacked Jesus, denouncing His teachings and finally attributing His miracles to the power of Beelzebub (Satan). This prompted the Lord's statement that their sins of unbelief were unpardonable. Actually, the attribution of any of God's work to any other source—whether it be another god, or chance (as in the theory of evolution), or the current favorite, self—is blasphemy and therefore a sin (**Isaiah 42:8**). What makes sin unpardonable is the refusal to accept the remedy God has provided in His Son, which is what they were doing.

Matthew 13 opens with the "time stamp" that places this teaching later that same day, so we'll expect to find some expansion of His statement about unpardonable sin. And although they're sometimes called the Seven Kingdom Parables, there are only six that begin with the phrase "the Kingdom of Heaven is like ..." The first parable describes the world in general.

A parable, as you now know, is a Heavenly story put into an Earthly context. The meaning of the Greek word for **parable** is *to place alongside,* as in a comparison. This means everything in the parable symbolizes something else. Correctly interpreting the symbols is the key that unlocks understanding. Some think of parables simply as marvelous teaching tools, but when the disciples asked Jesus why He taught in parables, He told them that His purpose was twofold: to enlighten believers, while at the same time confusing unbelievers (**Matthew 13:11-15**). And in fact, there has been much confusion among commentators in correctly interpreting the symbols of the Kingdom Parables, as we'll see.

To begin with, Matthew's use of the word **Heaven** in the parables has led some Gentile theologians off the track. I believe Matthew wrote His Gospel to Jews to convince them that Jesus was their Messiah. The use of the word **God** is avoided in Judaism to preclude breaking a commandment, and even today Jewish writers will often leave out the vowel, writing G-d to avoid offending Him. I think Matthew substituted the word Heaven for God in consideration of his Jewish readers. Some have also equated the phrase Kingdom of Heaven with the Church, which I believe is another error we'll discover.

ONE FINAL NOTE

Keep in mind that Jesus was speaking to Jews in Israel engaged in an agrarian economy and so it's logical that we should try and replicate their perspective in understanding the symbols He used. Since His listeners were only familiar with their Scriptures, we'll rely on the Old Testament as our theological guide, and since most worked the land, we'll use our knowledge of agriculture to give us the proper context.

1) The Parable of the Sower

 A farmer went out to sow his seed. As he was

scattering his seed some fell along the path and the birds came and ate it up. Some fell on rocky places where it did not have much soil. It sprang up quickly because the soil was shallow but when the sun came up the plants were scorched and they withered because they had no root. Other seed fell among thorns, which grew up and choked the plants. Still others fell on good soil where it produced a crop a hundred, sixty, or thirty times what was sown. He who has ears let him hear. (**Matthew 13:3-9**)

In this first parable the farmer's field symbolizes the world, and the seed is His Word sown throughout the Age of Man. The four kinds of soil describe mankind's various responses to His Word and the birds represent Satan. We know this because the Lord Himself interpreted this parable for us.

 Listen then to what the parable of the sower means: When anyone hears the message about the kingdom and does not understand it, the evil one comes and snatches away what was sown in their heart. This is the seed sown on the path. The one who received the seed that fell on rocky places is the man who hears the word and at once receives it with joy. But since he has no root it lasts only a short time. When trouble or persecution comes because of the word, they quickly fall away. The one who received the seed that fell among the thorns refers to someone who hears the word but the worries of this life and the deceitfulness of wealth choke it making it unfruitful. But the seed falling on good soil refers to someone who hears the word and understands it. This is the one who produces a crop yielding a hundred or sixty or thirty times what was sown. (**Matthew 13:18-23**)

His explanation is critical to us because of a principle of interpretation called "Expositional Constancy" which holds that symbolism tends to be consistent in Scripture. And so, the Lord's explanation of His symbolism in the first parable helps us understand the others. You'll find that some commentators violate this principle in interpreting the Kingdom Parables because they don't like what it tells them. We'll avoid that trap.

2) The Parable of the Weeds

> 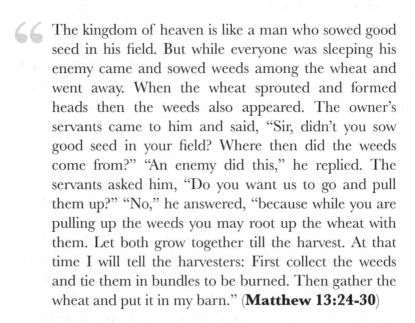 The kingdom of heaven is like a man who sowed good seed in his field. But while everyone was sleeping his enemy came and sowed weeds among the wheat and went away. When the wheat sprouted and formed heads then the weeds also appeared. The owner's servants came to him and said, "Sir, didn't you sow good seed in your field? Where then did the weeds come from?" "An enemy did this," he replied. The servants asked him, "Do you want us to go and pull them up?" "No," he answered, "because while you are pulling up the weeds you may root up the wheat with them. Let both grow together till the harvest. At that time I will tell the harvesters: First collect the weeds and tie them in bundles to be burned. Then gather the wheat and put it in my barn." (**Matthew 13:24-30**)

The Lord also interpreted this parable for us in verses 37-43. Here again, the Farmer is the Lord, and the field is the world. This time the good seed is further clarified as the effect His Word has had on some men (sons of the Kingdom), while the bad seed describes the effect Satan has had on others (sons of the evil one). This is additional proof that the Lord is describing the Age of Man where good and evil dwell side by side, and where the battle still continues for men's souls. Please note: there are only two kinds of seed in the field indicating that there have only been two kinds of people on Earth— sons of the Kingdom and sons of the evil one. We're all one or the other. At the end of the age, the Lord will send out his angels to "weed out of His Kingdom everything that causes sin and all who do evil. They will throw them into the fiery furnace where there will be weeping and gnashing of teeth. Then the righteous will shine like the sun in the kingdom of their father." (**Matthew 13:41-43**)

THAT WAS YOUR FIRST MISTAKE

Some Christians use this parable to defend a post-Tribulation Rapture position for the Church, but the description of events doesn't match other descriptions of the Rapture. He doesn't send out angels to gather His Church, He comes Himself (**1 Thessalonians 4:16**). Also, there are those in His Kingdom who aren't part of the Church. There are Old Testament Believers who died in faith of a coming Messiah but didn't live to see the events of the cross (see chapter 47). They're part of His Kingdom. And then there are the Tribulation Saints who come to faith after the Rapture and are martyred during the Great Tribulation. They're part of His Kingdom too. Just because these parables are in the Gospels doesn't mean they apply only to the Church, so using them to support a position unique to the Church takes them out of context. The Great Tribulation takes place on Earth. Its purpose is to judge the nations and purify Israel (**Jeremiah 30:1-11**) before bringing surviving believers into His Kingdom. The order and description of events in this parable fit that purpose. Then there's the problem that the doctrine of the Rapture wasn't introduced on Earth until after the Lord's death (**1 Thessalonians 4:16-17 & 1 Corinthians 15:51-52**) for reasons explained in **1 Corinthians 2:7-10.**

Our method of interpretation requires a literal, historical, and grammatical view of Scripture. It means we can't take this or any other passage out of context to support a preconceived position or apply it only from the narrow confines of our own perspective. The Bible cannot contradict itself. Things either fit, or they don't. Next, we'll see how the parables of the Mustard Seed and the Yeast have been twisted to produce an entirely inaccurate picture of God's Kingdom on Earth during the Age of Man.

3) The Parable of the Mustard Seed

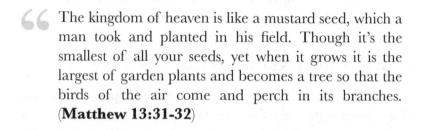

> The kingdom of heaven is like a mustard seed, which a man took and planted in his field. Though it's the smallest of all your seeds, yet when it grows it is the largest of garden plants and becomes a tree so that the birds of the air come and perch in its branches. (**Matthew 13:31-32**)

Here is one of the most apt descriptions of the Lord's Kingdom on Earth. A small seed is planted that should grow into a large garden plant. But this seed grows into something it was never intended to be, a tree so big that birds come to perch in it. Some commentators equate this with the incredible growth of the Church, but that violates both the agricultural context and the principle of Expositional Constancy I referred to before. Mustard seeds don't become trees, so something has gone wrong. And, as the Lord explained in His interpretation of the first parable, the birds represent the Evil One (**Matthew 13:19**). So this parable really predicts something quite different about Church growth. Remember, the seed is His Word, and the field is the world. He planted His Word in the world and as it grew it was perverted into something it was never intended to be—man-made bureaucracies so large that even Satan could find a place there.

Well if this interpretation has merit we should find evidence in Scripture to support it. Let's try **Isaiah 29:13** for starters: "These people come near to me with their mouth and honor me with their lips, but their hearts are far from me. Their worship of me is made up only of rules taught by men." In both Ezekiel and Jeremiah, He laments that their worship has become so perverted as to make Him sick (**Jeremiah 6:16-21**).

"But that's the Old Testament," you say, "Surely the Church is different." Read **2 Corinthians 10:13-15**: "For such men are false apostles, deceitful workmen masquerading as apostles of Christ. And no wonder, for Satan himself masquerades as an angel of light. It is not surprising then if his servants masquerade as servants of righteousnes*s*." Just as the Lord is the same yesterday today and forever, so are people.

4) The Parable of the Yeast

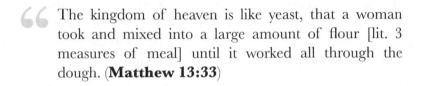

The kingdom of heaven is like yeast, that a woman took and mixed into a large amount of flour [lit. 3 measures of meal] until it worked all through the dough. (**Matthew 13:33**)

Some also interpret this parable as describing the way the Gospel has spread throughout the world, but it's really another way of saying the same thing as the previous one. Again, our search for clues takes us to the only Scriptures they had, the Old Testament.

The first one is in **Genesis 18**, where Abraham unexpectedly found himself entertaining three visitors. Even before he realized who they were, (the visitors turned out to be the Lord and two angels on their way to Sodom and Gomorrah) he had Sarah and the servants quickly prepare some food and drink as a sign of hospitality. As you read the passage, note Abraham's admonitions to hurry. You can't quickly bake bread unless you're making unleavened bread, the kind without yeast. Otherwise, it takes several hours. This quickly prepared meal became a tradition in the Middle East, known as the friendship offering, and was incorporated into the Temple Ceremony as the Grain Offering. Unleavened bread was prescribed for both offerings.

When the Lord mentioned the inclusion of yeast in the friendship offering to His Jewish audience, they realized once again that He was describing something that shouldn't happen. This time, the one in charge, the woman, was deliberately including an undesirable ingredient. But what's the significance of yeast? Well, in the Old

Testament yeast can be seen as a symbol for sin (**Exodus 34:25**). Specifically, it came to signify the sin of pride because of their similar properties. Yeast begins a corruption process when mixed with flour and water, causing the dough to swell as it ferments. Pride does the same to us, hence the adage, "swelling with pride."

By removing all the yeast from their households before Passover, Jewish families symbolically rid themselves of sin in preparation for celebrating their deliverance from Egypt (**Exodus 12:15**). The Lord Jesus, our Passover Lamb, took away our sin in preparation for our deliverance from Earth. Even most liberal Christian commentators today agree that every time yeast is used symbolically (except here, they say) it's used to symbolize sin. Expositional Constancy.

Using these clues then, our adherence to both the context of the parable and the principle of Expositional Constancy requires an interpretation consistent with the Parable of the Mustard Seed. While on Earth, the Kingdom of Heaven will be infested with sin, often with the help of the very leaders sworn to protect and preserve it, something that makes it unsuitable for God. We can't remove the sin from ourselves any more than the dough can remove the yeast from its midst. The unpardonable sin is rejecting the Lord's solution to our problem because by doing so we place ourselves beyond His reach. (His shed blood is the only sin remedy He has provided.) By rejecting His remedy, we've also allied ourselves with God's enemy Satan, because as the Parable of the Weeds (2) explained, there are only two sides to this battle and there are no neutrals. This has been true since the inception of the Kingdom of Heaven in its Earthly phase and will remain so till He removes us to our permanent place of residence. And that's the topic of the next two parables.

5) The Hidden Treasure

 The kingdom of heaven is like treasure hidden in a field. When a man found it, he hid it again, and then in his joy went and sold all that he had and bought the field. (**Matthew 13:44**)

Following the Principle of Expositional Constancy, where the symbolic use of things in Scripture tends to be consistent, we know from the first three parables that the man is the Lord, and the field is the world. He found a treasure in the world but didn't remove it. Instead, He gave everything He had to purchase the whole world, just to get the treasure.

When the Lord created Adam, He gave him dominion over the whole world (**Genesis 1:28**). Adam subsequently lost it to Satan, and that's why Satan is called the prince of this world (**John 12:31, 14:30, & 16:11**) and the god of this age (**2 Corinthians 4:4**). Later the Lord discovered a hidden treasure in the world but didn't remove it. Instead, He came to Earth as a man and gave His life (everything He had), redeeming the whole world to gain the treasure.

In **Exodus 19:5**, **Deuteronomy 7:6**, and **Malachi 3:17** Israel is described as God's treasure. No other people are given this distinction. The history and destiny of Israel has always been tied to the world, and the Lord gave His life to redeem her. In the Millennium Israel is restored to her former glory and once again becomes the pre-eminent nation on Earth, God's treasured possession.

6) The Pearl of Great Price

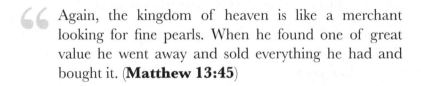
Again, the kingdom of heaven is like a merchant looking for fine pearls. When he found one of great value he went away and sold everything he had and bought it. (**Matthew 13:45**)

Some see this as just a continuation of the previous parable— another way of saying the same thing. In a way that's true, but there is one huge difference. Pearls come from oysters, which are not "kosher." Oysters, having neither fins nor scales, were forbidden for Israel (**Leviticus 11:10-12**) and so pearls were not prized by them as they were by Gentiles. Pearls are distinctly Gentile in nature and in many ways the formation and ultimate destiny of a pearl is remarkably similar to that of the Church.

A pearl is the only gem derived from a living organism, formed in response to an irritant. Somehow a grain of sand gets lodged inside an oyster shell irritating its flesh. Unable to remove the irritant, the oyster secretes a fluid that hardens around the sand forming a smooth round ball relieving the irritation. We call this hardened round ball a pearl. When the oyster is harvested, the pearl is removed from its natural habitat to become an object of adornment.

The Church is a living organism that has always experienced its most dramatic growth as a response to persecution. One day soon, the Lord will come and remove His Church from the world, her natural habitat, to make her His bride, the object of His affection.

Don't be fooled by some commentators who use these parables to teach that the Kingdom is both the treasure and the pearl and we should be willing to give everything we have to purchase our place in it. That view violates the context and intent of the parables and is theologically unfounded. We have nothing God needs. In His sight, we are totally without merit or substance, unable to purchase anything from Him. Entry into the Kingdom is free for the asking because the Lord gave everything He had to make it so. God made Him who had no sin to be sin for us so that in Him we might become the righteousness of God (**2 Corinthians 5:21**).

In these two parables then, we see the destinies of both Israel and the Church symbolized. In Jewish eschatology, the Lord promised to return and live among them in His Holy Land, the land He promised to Abraham, Isaac, and Jacob: the land of Israel (**Ezekiel 40-48**). In Christian eschatology, we are promised that one day the Lord will come to take us to be with Him in Heaven (**John 14:1-3**). As the treasure is left in the field, Israel is left in the world. As the pearl is removed from the oyster, the Church is removed from the Earth. In both cases the Lord impoverished Himself to purchase that which He desired, giving each the destiny He promised.

BUT WAIT A MINUTE

There's a phrase in **Matthew 13:44** that is often overlooked but has always astonished me. "In his joy he went and sold everything he had." On the night of His betrayal, Scriptures tell us, that after their meal Jesus and the disciples sang a hymn, and went out to the Garden of Gethsemane at the foot of the Mount of Olives (**Matthew 26:30**). There He would be betrayed, arrested, and subjected to the most intense humiliation and deprivation. And finally, beaten within an inch of His life before dying the most painful death known to man. All of this would happen within the span of the day just begun, for the Jewish day begins at sunset, and by the following sunset He would be in the grave. Of course, He knew this from the beginning (**Matthew 26:52-54**).

By tradition, the hymn sung following the Passover meal comes from **Psalm 118:22-24**:

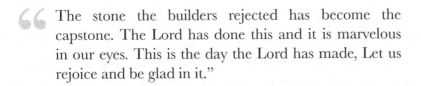

> The stone the builders rejected has become the capstone. The Lord has done this and it is marvelous in our eyes. This is the day the Lord has made, Let us rejoice and be glad in it."

This was the day, ordained from before the foundation of the world. The day when, by agreement, the Son of God would become the Redeemer of Israel and beyond that a Light for the Gentiles to bring God's salvation to the ends of the Earth (**Isaiah 49:5-6**). This was the day when He would pay the required price to purchase His Bride, and when He would make possible the reconciliation between God and His Creation (**Colossians 1:19-20**). Even His knowledge of the torment, anguish, and pain He would endure was not enough to diminish the joy He felt at being able to give the greatest gift of love ever given. He sang, *"This is the day the Lord has made, let us rejoice and be glad in it."*

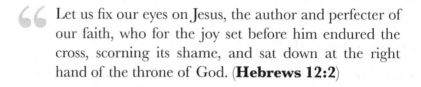 Let us fix our eyes on Jesus, the author and perfecter of our faith, who for the joy set before him endured the cross, scorning its shame, and sat down at the right hand of the throne of God. (**Hebrews 12:2**)

7) The Parable of the Net

Once again, the kingdom of heaven is like a net that was let down into the lake and caught all kinds of fish. When it was full the fishermen pulled it up on the shore. Then they sat down and collected the good fish in baskets and threw the bad fish away. This is how it will be at the end of the age. The angels will come and separate the wicked from the righteous and throw them into the fiery furnace where there will be weeping and gnashing of teeth. (**Matthew 13:47-50**)

EXPOSITIONAL CONSTANCY

Throughout the Old Testament, when the sea is used symbolically, it refers to the Gentile world. For example, when the Lord described the reign of Gentile Kingdoms that began with Babylon and would continue to the end of the age, He pictured them as voracious beasts that came out of the sea (**Daniel 7**). During the Lord's time on Earth, the region surrounding the Sea of Galilee was called "Galilee of the Nations" or "Galilee of the Gentiles" (same Hebrew word) because of the size of the Gentile population in the area. The phrase comes from **Isaiah 9:1**, a passage that introduces the coming of the Messiah. Some commentators see this parable then, as being particularly Gentile in its focus. They also make a big deal out of the fact that He used fish to symbolize people and fishermen to symbolize angels. They jump to the conclusion that He must be describing the Church since the Church later took the fish as a symbol and the several disciples were fishermen.

As we read the story, it's tempting to agree and see the Church being symbolized in the fish, and pre-trib believers note with glee that the order is correct. The good fish are collected before the bad are thrown into the fiery furnace (Great Tribulation, they say). But I think He was sitting there overlooking the sea surrounded by folks who made their living from it and using common everyday activities well known to them to make His point. And these activities don't match other descriptions of the Rapture, where the Lord Himself comes to gather up His Church (**1 Thessalonians 4:16-17**). And then there's the issue of other believers, not part of the Church, who belong in the kingdom as well. We discussed these earlier.

But the biggest problem in equating the fish and the Church is the fact that in the parable some are good and some are bad, which the Lord described as symbolizing the righteous and the unrighteous. If you're in the Church, you're as righteous as God Himself (**2 Corinthians 5:17-21**) His righteousness having been imputed to you when you accepted the pardon His death purchased for you.

In God's eyes, there are no unrighteous believers. True, the case has been made that many who go to church have never really been born again, but that's a point based on our definition of the Church, not the Lord's. Membership in His Church is gained by accepting His death as payment for our sins, not by external actions like attendance or donation records, or even evidence of "good works." He's not fooled by such behavior since He knows the motives of our hearts.

From His point of view, we're either in or we're not—there's no middle ground. So the fish have to represent humanity at large, Jew and Gentile, present on Earth at the end of the age, the time to which the Lord refers in the parable.

THE STORY THAT EXPLAINS THE STORY

In **Matthew 25:31-46** the Lord gave a teaching that describes a judgment He'll conduct directly after the Great Tribulation and His subsequent return to Earth in glory with all the angels. All of surviving humanity, He said, will be divided into two groups, one called "sheep" and the other "goats." The sheep are positioned on His right and the goats on His left. The sheep are rewarded for their faith, as evidenced by their attitude toward "His brothers" during their recent time of trouble, by being ushered into His Kingdom. The goats are then condemned to the eternal fires for ignoring His brothers.

I believe His brothers are Jewish believers who will be hunted like dogs during the Great Tribulation in Satan's last great effort to annihilate them and prevent the Lord's return. The sheep are Gentiles who come to faith after the Rapture and who, at great personal risk, provide for and comfort them. The goats are those who refuse to love the truth and be saved (**2 Thessalonians 2:9-12**) and therefore see no reason to help believers of any stripe, especially Jews. (Note that sheep are always used symbolically to describe believers, while the goat's head is a traditional symbol of Satan.)

Clearly, in the Sheep and Goat Judgment humanity will be assigned to one group or the other based upon righteousness. The implication in the passage is that the angels are involved in gathering all of surviving humanity together for this judgment, the sheep are first commended and rewarded, and then the goats are consigned to the eternal fire. Sounds just like the Parable of the Net.

FROM GENESIS TO REVELATION

 Therefore every teacher of the Law who has been instructed about the kingdom of heaven is like the owner of the house who brings out of his storeroom new treasures as well as old. (**Matthew 13:52**)

This is the clearest indication of all that His Kingdom will contain believers from every segment of the Age of Man, not just the Church. This concluding statement ties the New Testament with the Old and indicates that those who have been led by the Holy Spirit to teach the Scriptures would hereafter include the whole counsel of God, from Genesis to Revelation.

IN CONCLUSION

Here then is a summary of God's redemptive work during the Age of Man, with man's response to it as illustrated by the seven parables:

The Lord has planted the seed of His Word throughout the world in both Old Testament and New, proclaiming His Kingdom (1). Satan has worked to prevent and pervert His Word (2-3), often getting able assistance from the very leaders sworn on holy oath to protect and preserve it (4). His Kingdom was always intended for both Jew and Gentile and He gave all He had, including His life, so we could escape the bondage of sin and join Him there (5-6). But loving us enough to give us the freedom to accept or reject the only remedy available for the sin that bars our admission meant that many would refuse His offer of pardon to their own destruction (7).

In **Matthew 25:41** we're told that the eternal fires were prepared specifically for Satan and his angels. People must choose to join them there. By refusing the Lord's offer of pardon and thereby rejecting His kingdom, they choose the only other destiny available, joining Satan in his. This is the one and only unpardonable sin.

Now you know the adult version.

CHAPTER THIRTY-EIGHT

JESUS CALMS THE STORM

DON'T YOU CARE IF WE DROWN?

> Then he got into the boat and his disciples followed him. Without warning, a furious storm came up on the lake, so that the waves swept over the boat. But Jesus was sleeping. The disciples went and woke him, saying, "Lord, save us! We're going to drown!"
>
> He replied, "You of little faith, why are you so afraid?" Then he got up and rebuked the winds and the waves, and it was completely calm. The men were amazed and asked, "What kind of man is this? Even the winds and the waves obey him!" (**Matthew 8:23-27**)

It was another one of those days where the crowds followed them everywhere. All day, Jesus had been healing the sick and teaching them about the cost of following Him. Finally, they got into a boat and began to cross the Sea of Galilee when suddenly one of those storms that seem to come out of nowhere was right on top of them.

The Sea of Galilee is noted for these. The way the hills to the east are formed sometimes creates a Venturi effect when the wind blows just right, and unexpected storms materialize very quickly.

But remember, these disciples were fishermen. They made their living on this lake and had seen just about every kind of weather imaginable. This was no ordinary storm, and they were afraid for their lives.

WHAT'S GOING ON HERE?

Here was a classic case of spiritual harassment. The enemy knew he couldn't defeat the Lord this way, and even if one of the disciples wound up going overboard and drowning, Jesus could bring him back to life. I say the enemy knew this, but the disciples didn't. They were still pretty new at this and the storm terrified them. They couldn't imagine how the Lord slept through it all. "Lord, save us!" they said. "We're going to drown!"

He got up, calmed the storm with a word, and rebuked them for their lack of faith. In hindsight, this looks to us like a logical thing to do. After all, how could something like a freak storm derail the plans He and His Father had made before the creation of the world? He certainly wasn't going to lose any of them by sleeping through a crucial moment. Nothing could or would happen to them as long as they were in His presence.

But they were just ordinary folks, working class men. What did they know about spiritual warfare or opposing cosmic forces? They hadn't even been given the Holy Spirit yet. And their amazement at His authority over the wind shows they still thought of Him as an ordinary man.

So they had a plausible excuse for their lack of faith, but the story was written for us. For everything that was written in the past was written to teach us, so that through endurance and the encouragement of the Scriptures we might have hope (**Romans 15:4**). We have been given the Holy Spirit to guide us into all understanding.

And in His Word, the Lord promised to be with us always, to never leave or forsake us, and for 2,000 years He's proven Himself faithful. He promised that He who began a good work in us will carry it on to completion until the day of Christ Jesus (**Philippians 1:6**). What's our excuse for crying out in a moment of uncertainty and fear? Don't we deserve the same rebuke? "You of little faith, why are you so afraid?"

Now you know the adult version.

CHAPTER THIRTY-NINE

FEEDING THE 5,000

THE WORLD'S FIRST FAST FOOD MEAL

> As evening approached the disciples came to him and said, "This is a remote place and it's already getting late. Send the crowds away so they can go to the villages and buy themselves some food." Jesus replied, "They do not need to go away. You give them something to eat." "We have here only five loaves of bread and two fish," they answered. "Bring them here to me," he said. And he directed the people to sit down on the grass. Taking the five loaves and the two fish and looking up to heaven he gave thanks and broke the loaves. Then he gave them to the disciples and the disciples gave them to the people. They all ate and were satisfied and the disciples picked up twelve basketfuls of broken pieces that were left over. The number of those who ate was about 5000 men besides women and children. (**Matthew 14:15-21**)

I'M ONLY GOING TO SAY THIS FOUR TIMES

This is the only miracle Jesus performed before His Resurrection that is included in all the Gospels, and so it must be important. Reading all four accounts (the one from Matthew above plus **Mark 6:32-44**, **Luke 9:10-17**, and **John 6:1-13**) is necessary to gain the full impact of the story because each writer included details unique to his version.

(For my article on the need for four Gospel accounts, read The Four Faces of Jesus at gracethrufaith.com.)

The basic premise is laid out in Matthew. There were 5,000 men, plus an undetermined number of women and children, who had followed Jesus into a remote spot having heard He was in the area. (Remember it was only the Jewish Leadership that rejected Him. He was enormously popular with the people. That's one of the reasons the leaders feared Him.) Some of the disciples became concerned as evening approached that the people would be hungry and there wouldn't be anything to give them. They had located five barley loaves and two fish, only enough for one or two people. But when Jesus took what they had and gave thanks for it, it became more than enough to feed the entire crowd. Twelve baskets full of pieces were left over, more than they had started with.

LOOK FOR THE HIDDEN MEANING

The Feeding of the 5,000 turns out to be as important symbolically as it is factually. The numbers given in these accounts are spiritually significant. (I encourage you to undertake a study of the Biblical use of numbers. *Number in Scripture*, a book by E.W. Bullinger, is a good reference to help get you started.) When the number five is used, you'll often find that it's within the context of a manifestation of the Grace of God, and two is the number of witness (**Deuteronomy 19:15**). Twelve is the number of government and often refers to Israel as well. Add to these the fact that Jesus identified Himself as the Bread of Life given for us (**John 6:35**), and that the fish became the symbol for believers in His Word, a name also used of Him (**John 1:1**), and the hidden message begins to emerge.

With these insights, we can see the message Jesus was sending, "By the Grace of God you'll be spiritually fed as the Bread of Life gives Himself to you. The witness of His Word will sustain you and enough of the Bread of Life will be given for all the House of Israel." Jesus likened this miracle to the giving of the manna in the wilderness, indicating that it was a foreshadowing of Him (**John 6:25-40**).

LET'S SEE YOU DO THAT AGAIN

By the way, on another occasion, Jesus miraculously fed 4,000 men plus women and children (**Matthew 15:29-31, Mark 8:1-10**). There they found seven loaves and a few small fish among the crowd. Again, Jesus made it sufficient for all, and there were seven baskets full left over. Four is the number of the Earth (on day four the land and sea were separated), and seven denotes divine completion, for on the seventh day the creation was finished and God rested from all His work. Here the symbolism denotes that Jesus was giving Himself to all the Earth and there is plenty for everyone's spiritual hunger to be completely satisfied. Many scholars see this miracle being Gentile in focus while the feeding of 5,000 is aimed at Israel. Put the two together and see that there's enough of Him for all the world, Jew and Gentile alike. The Feeding of the 4,000 is included in only two Gospels, a witness to both Jew and Gentile.

BACK TO THE 5,000

In his account of this miracle, Mark describes the crowd as being "like sheep without a shepherd." (**Mark 6:34**) And he mentions that the grass upon which the people were made to sit was green, recalling the phrase from **Psalm 23**, "*He makes me lie down in green* *pastures."* And indeed **Psalm 23** describes how the Good Shepherd tends His flock. Mark also inserts an additional use of the number five, describing how the people were organized into groups of 100s and 50s. And incredibly, Mark hints that the disciples actually had enough money with them to buy dinner for the entire group (**Mark 6:37**). So much for the notion that Jesus and His disciples were penniless vagabonds living off the land.

Luke adds what I think is the most fascinating piece of information of all: the location of the miracle. It was near a town called Bethsaida. The name is usually translated *house of fishing* and denotes their proximity to the Sea of Galilee and the town's major industry. But the Hebrew root words making up Bethsaida provide real insight into God's sense of humor. **Beth** is Hebrew for *house*, and **sayid** literally means *box lunch*. This miraculous and instantaneous feeding took place near the "House of the Box Lunch" and was perhaps the real origin of the fast food industry (just kidding).

John says the event took place near the time of the Jewish Passover, explaining why the grass was green (it was spring time) and lets us in on what Jesus was thinking. Would His disciples who knew Him better than anyone suggest that He had the supernatural power to feed them all or propose a merely human solution? How like us they were. With all the power of the universe in their midst, they could only devise a response based on their own capability (**John 6:5-9**).

John also gives us the crowd's reaction. "Surely this is the Prophet Who is to come into the world," they said. Jesus, knowing they intended to come and make Him king by force, withdrew again to a mountain by Himself (**John 6:14-15**). They didn't understand that Jesus needed to fulfill His role as the Obedient Servant by first dying for their sins before accepting His destiny as King of Kings. Later He accused them of only following Him because He fed them (**John 6:26**). Sounds like us again.

A LESSON IN NUTRITION

And so in these miraculous feedings, we see the Gospel story told in a truly practical manner. By giving us His Son, our God brings life to all His people, Jew and Gentile, completely satisfying our spiritual hunger and sustaining us through the power of His Word. Interesting that bread is a carbohydrate, a type of food that instantly energizes us, while fish, being protein gives us staying power.

Now you know the adult version.

CHAPTER FORTY

JESUS WALKS ON WATER

IT JUST TAKES FAITH

> Immediately Jesus made the disciples get into the boat and go on ahead of him to the other side, while he dismissed the crowd. After he had dismissed them, he went up on a mountainside by himself to pray. When evening came he was there alone but the boat was already a considerable distance from land, buffeted by the waves because the wind was against it. During the fourth watch of the night Jesus went out to them, walking on the lake. When the disciples saw him walking on the lake they were terrified. "It's a ghost," they said, and cried out in fear. But Jesus immediately said to them, "Take courage. It is I. Don't be afraid." **(Matthew 14:22-27)**

This story appears in **Mark 6:45-51** and **John 6:15-21,** and as in the Feeding of the 5,000 lots of additional insight can be gained by comparing all the accounts. All agree that this event followed immediately on the heels of the miraculous feeding and that the disciples set out across the lake without Jesus, while He went up the mountainside alone to pray.

If you read the preamble to the Feeding of the 5,000, you'll recall that Jesus came to that remote area to be alone with His disciples to grieve the death of John the Baptist and hear the reports of their recent missionary tour. But their presence was discovered, and they were followed by a huge group of people (**Matthew 14:13-14 & Mark 6:30**). Putting aside His own needs, He ministered to the crowd, fed and dismissed them, and was now free to be alone. Perhaps sending the disciples out without Him was even an effort to divert the crowd and get some "face time" with His Father. John the Baptist was a relative (**Luke 1:36**) and had just been beheaded by Herod as a favor to his wife (**Matthew 14:1-12**), and the 12 had just completed their first assignment, spreading the Gospel throughout Israel. It was time to check in.

MOVEMENT WITHOUT PROGRESS

From **Matthew 14:25** we learn it was the fourth watch of the night (3-6 a.m.). And from John's account we learn the disciples had only covered about 3-3.5 miles (half the distance across the lake) yet they had been rowing since early evening (**John 6:19**). They were straining at the oars but not getting very far. In fact, Mark tells us Jesus was making better time walking on the water than they were rowing and He was about to pass them by when they saw Him, even though they had a head start of several hours (**Mark 6:48**).

Thinking He was a ghost they were terrified. But Jesus calmed them by identifying Himself. "Take courage. It is I. Don't be afraid." By the way, the words translated "It is I" in verse 27 can also be translated "I am," the same words spoken to Moses from the burning bush.

 "Lord, if it's you," Peter replied, "Tell me to come to you on the water." "Come," he said. Then Peter got

down out of the boat, walked on the water and came
toward Jesus. But when he saw the wind he was afraid,
and beginning to sink cried out, "Lord, save me."
Immediately Jesus reached out his hand and caught
him. "You of little faith," he said. "why did you
doubt?" And when they climbed into the boat the
wind died down. Then those who were in the boat
worshiped him, saying, "Truly, you are the Son of
God." (**Matthew 14:28-33**)

His mastery over the laws of nature had persuaded them.

LET'S GET MYSTICAL

Here is one of the truly remarkable bits of New Covenant
symbolism to be found anywhere in Scripture. Let the boat and
disciples represent Israel, the Sea the unbelieving world (**Isaiah
57:20-21**) and Peter the Church. I'll use the term Church here to
mean anything from a single believer to the entire body of Christ, so
it's OK to take this personally as well as institutionally.

As the disciples had made very little progress rowing across the sea
against the wind, Israel had made very little progress in their
mandate to tell the world about God (**Isaiah 43:10-13**). And as
Peter was called out of the boat to walk on the water, the Church
was called out of Israel to dwell in the world and spread the Gospel
(**Matthew 28:19-20**).

As long as Peter stayed focused on the Lord he was able to remain
above the waves, empowered by his faith to perform a miracle and
sustained by his closeness to the Lord. When he was distracted by
the winds, he began to sink, and his life was in peril. As long as we
stay focused on the Lord, we're able to remain above the ways of
this world, empowered by our faith to perform miraculous works
and sustained by our closeness to Him. When we're distracted by
the winds of controversy and deceit, we begin sinking into the
world's unbelieving ways, and our spiritual life is in peril.

When Peter cried out, "Lord save me," the Lord was immediately at his side, reaching out to rescue him and bring him to safety. When we cry out, "Lord save me," the Lord is immediately at our side, reaching out to rescue us and bring us to safety. We are never beyond His reach.

One more point. When Peter and the Lord got safely back into the boat, the wind died down and calm returned. When Israel and the Church are finally reunited in Christ, peace will reign in the world. In both cases the Lord's gentle rebuke to Peter is appropriate. To both Israel and the Church He says, "You of little faith, why did you doubt?"

Now you know the adult version.

CHAPTER FORTY-ONE

THE UNMERCIFUL SERVANT

WHAT GOES AROUND COMES AROUND

> Then Peter came to Jesus and asked, "Lord, how many times shall I forgive my brother when he sins against me? Up to seven times?"

Jesus answered, "I tell you, not seven times, but seventy-seven times. (Or seventy times seven)

"Therefore, the kingdom of heaven is like a king who wanted to settle accounts with his servants. As he began the settlement, a man who owed him ten thousand talents was brought to him. Since he was not able to pay, the master ordered that he and his wife and his children and all that he had be sold to repay the debt.

"The servant fell on his knees before him. 'Be patient with me,' he begged, 'and I will pay back everything.' The servant's master took pity on him, canceled the debt and let him go.

"But when that servant went out, he found one of his fellow servants who owed him a hundred denarii. He grabbed him and began to choke him. 'Pay back what you owe me!' he demanded.

"His fellow servant fell to his knees and begged him, 'Be patient with me, and I will pay you back.'

"But he refused. Instead, he went off and had the man thrown into prison until he could pay the debt. When the other servants saw what had happened, they were greatly distressed and went and told their master everything that had happened.

"Then the master called the servant in. 'You wicked servant,' he said, 'I canceled all that debt of yours because you begged me to. Shouldn't you have had mercy on your fellow servant just as I had on you?' In anger his master turned him over to the jailers to be tortured, until he should pay back all he owed.

"This is how my heavenly Father will treat each of you unless you forgive your brother from your heart." (**Matthew 18:21-35**)

THE REST OF THE STORY

Most people have read the first part of **Matthew 18**. It outlines a procedure for taking to task a believer who has sinned against you. Many an aggressive stance has been justified with this passage. But in my time as a pastor and counselor, I was surprised at how few of those applying the procedure had read the rest of the chapter. While chapter breaks are not inspired, and Peter's question to the Lord about forgiveness (vs. 21) could have been asked at another time, it does appear next in sequence to the procedure for righting a wrong.

How many petty disputes could be dropped if put into the context of this parable? How would they rate in a comparison to what the Lord has forgiven us? Do we, having been forgiven so much, refuse to forgive our brothers and sisters even a little? And if so, what are the real consequences?

We've often discussed the nature of parables: how they're Heavenly stories put into an Earthly context and how the major characters always symbolize others. In the case of this parable, the King is the Lord, you and I are His servants, the debts we owe represent our sins, and the jailer is Satan.

Identifying the King and his servants is easy. As to the debts owed, two denominations of money are mentioned, the 10,000 talents the servant owed the king and the 100 denarii the servant was owed by another. Let's take the easy one first. Almost everyone agrees that a denarius was equivalent to one day's wages. If 100 days equaled about one third of a working year then repaying that size debt would require about four months of an average person's income. That's not an insignificant sum.

Since a talent was both a measure of weight (about 85 lbs. or 34 kg.) and a monetary coin, its value is harder to define, but the most frequent description I found in my research is that it would have approximated 15 times an average person's annual income. If so, then a debt of 10,000 talents would require 150,000 years of an average person's income to repay, an impossibly large amount.

And that's the first point. The King had forgiven a debt the servant couldn't have repaid in a hundred lifetimes and did so simply because he was asked. The servant, on the other hand, demanded full and immediate payment from a friend for a much, much smaller sum. Now four months wages is a debt worthy of collection, and forgiving an amount that size would be a major sacrifice for most people. But the issue is not the legitimacy or even the size of the debt, it's the comparative value. Shouldn't being released from the burden of a debt so large he could never repay it have made the servant even a little more forgiving toward his brother?

The servant's demand for payment demonstrated his lack of gratitude for what the King had done for him, and that's what aroused the King's anger. Summoning the Jailer, the King ordered his servant punished until he repaid all he owed.

IF THE SHOE FITS ...

Our debt of sin against the Lord is similarly impossible to repay, but in the Lord's case, He can't simply overlook it. His requirement for justice demands the debt be paid in full. Knowing we couldn't pay off this debt, even when given all eternity, He sent His Son to pay it for us. This freed Him to completely and unconditionally forgive us just because we ask Him to. Don't forget, from the Lord's point of view, with even the least of our sins, we were as culpable as murderers, adulterers, blasphemers and thieves. These are all crimes punishable by death. Yet He still forgave us (**Ephesians 2:1-5**).

Because we've been forgiven so much, isn't a significant sacrifice justifiable under the circumstances? What offense would be too large to forgive in others when compared with what the Lord has forgiven in us?

Our unwillingness to forgive legitimate sins our friends commit against us demonstrates our ingratitude for what the Lord has done for us. It's the result of the typical human double standard wherein we demand justice from others while expecting mercy for ourselves. This ingratitude is itself a sin and, like all unconfessed sin, leaves us open to attack by our enemy causing us great torment. See how the jailer represents Satan?

UNION AND FELLOWSHIP

Like the servant and the King, our relationship with the Lord consists of two components, union and fellowship. Just as the servant didn't stop being a servant to the King because of his bad behavior, neither do we ever stop being the children of our Lord. **That's union**.

The servant could restore himself to the King's good graces and stop the punishment by repaying the debt. We can restore ourselves to the Lord's good graces and stop the torment by applying the payment already made on our behalf for all our sins. "If we confess our sins, he is faithful and just and will forgive us our sins and purify us from all unrighteousness." (**1 John 1:9**) **That's fellowship.**

Please note that John was writing to forgiven sinners, members of the Church, advising us to confess and be forgiven even after we've been saved. We sin every day, and His mercies are new every morning. God forgives us whenever we ask, every time we ask. (For me that's been many more than seventy times seven.)

YOU ALWAYS GET WHAT YOU ASK FOR

God's Nature demands justice and fair play. Refusing to forgive when we've been forgiven causes a rift in our relationship with Him that only we can mend. Forgiving the friend who sinned against us, and asking the Lord to forgive us, restores us to fellowship with the Lord, and allows Him to forget there ever was a problem. And often, we'll discover that the torment we endured while out of fellowship will actually contain the seeds of a blessing once we return. Isn't that just like Him?

Now you know the adult version.

CHAPTER FORTY-TWO

THE LOST SHEEP, THE LOST COIN, AND THE LOST SON

THE PARABLE OF THE LOST SHEEP

> Then Jesus told them this parable: "Suppose one of you has a hundred sheep and loses one of them. Does he not leave the ninety-nine in the open country and go after the lost sheep until he finds it? And when he finds it, he joyfully puts it on his shoulders and goes home. Then he calls his friends and neighbors together and says, 'Rejoice with me; I have found my lost sheep.' I tell you that in the same way there will be more rejoicing in heaven over one sinner who repents than over ninety-nine righteous persons who do not need to repent."

THE PARABLE OF THE LOST COIN

> "Or suppose a woman has ten silver coins and loses one. Does she not light a lamp, sweep the house and

search carefully until she finds it? And when she finds it, she calls her friends and neighbors together and says, 'Rejoice with me; I have found my lost coin.' In the same way, I tell you, there is rejoicing in the presence of the angels of God over one sinner who repents."

THE PARABLE OF THE LOST SON (AKA THE PRODIGAL SON)

 Jesus continued: "There was a man who had two sons. The younger one said to his father, 'Father, give me my share of the estate.' So he divided his property between them.

"Not long after that, the younger son got together all he had, set off for a distant country and there squandered his wealth in wild living. After he had spent everything, there was a severe famine in that whole country, and he began to be in need. So he went and hired himself out to a citizen of that country, who sent him to his fields to feed pigs. He longed to fill his stomach with the pods that the pigs were eating, but no one gave him anything.

"When he came to his senses, he said, 'How many of my father's hired men have food to spare, and here I am starving to death! I will set out and go back to my father and say to him: Father, I have sinned against heaven and against you. I am no longer worthy to be called your son; make me like one of your hired men.' So he got up and went to his father.

"But while he was still a long way off, his father saw him and was filled with compassion for him; he ran to his son, threw his arms around him and kissed him.

"The son said to him, 'Father, I have sinned against heaven and against you. I am no longer worthy to be called your son.'

"But the father said to his servants, 'Quick! Bring the best robe and put it on him. Put a ring on his finger and sandals on his feet. Bring the fattened calf and kill it. Let's have a feast and celebrate. For this son of mine was dead and is alive again; he was lost and is found.' So they began to celebrate.

"Meanwhile, the older son was in the field. When he came near the house, he heard music and dancing. So he called one of the servants and asked him what was going on. 'Your brother has come,' he replied, 'and your father has killed the fattened calf because he has him back safe and sound.'

"The older brother became angry and refused to go in. So his father went out and pleaded with him. But he answered his father, 'Look! All these years I've been slaving for you and never disobeyed your orders. Yet you never gave me even a young goat so I could celebrate with my friends. But when this son of yours who has squandered your property with prostitutes comes home, you kill the fattened calf for him!'

"'My son,' the father said, 'you are always with me, and everything I have is yours. But we had to celebrate and be glad, because this brother of yours was dead and is alive again; he was lost and is found.'" (**Luke 15:3-32**)

WHAT'S GOING ON HERE?

The Pharisees and Teachers of the Law were muttering among themselves, criticizing the Lord for fraternizing with sinners. They believed that even acknowledging a sinner's presence was wrong, and sharing a meal with one was a sign of acceptance to be avoided at all costs. Guilt by association, they called it. It's an attitude that's still around. Go bankrupt, get a divorce, or even lose your job and you'll soon find out who your friends are. If you're lucky, one or two will come around. The rest will avoid you as if your condition is contagious and they might catch it.

The so-called righteous people of the day placed little or no value on the lives of sinners, believing their behavior had rendered them undeserving of any effort toward reconciliation. So Jesus told them three parables to explain God's view that sinners were actually of more urgent importance to Him than the righteous.

On one occasion He told them He had come to seek and save the lost (**Luke 19:10**), and on another that it was the sick who needed a doctor, not the healthy. "I have not come to call the righteous," He said, "but sinners to repentance." (**Luke 5:31-32**) Now He said, "If you had 100 sheep and one got lost you'd leave the 99 and search for the lost one wouldn't you? And wouldn't you be glad when you found it?"

"And suppose you had ten coins and lost one? Wouldn't you focus all your efforts on finding it? And when you did wouldn't you celebrate?"

If they felt that way about material possessions that could easily be replaced, how much more important should a human soul be?

To our Creator, each and every life is of infinite value—irreplaceable. He doesn't desire that any should perish, but that all would come to repentance (**2 Peter 3:9**). That's why there's more rejoicing in Heaven over redeeming one lost soul than over 99 who never got lost. And that's why every time a sinner repents and receives the Lord the angels in Heaven sing for joy.

By the way, the Bible only mentions five events that cause the angels to sing. One was when God said, "Let there be light," and the Earth came to life. Another was when the Lord Jesus was born. And another is when the Church arrives Heaven. And finally, the Lord's defeat of His enemies at the end of the age. That's just four other times in all the history of man. But they get plenty of practice because the fifth one repeats itself every time one of us comes to the Lord. In His view, saving a single life ranks right up there with creating and redeeming the world.

HERE'S THE POINT

But it's the third parable that must have cut them to the quick because it highlights the resentment the obedient son felt over the return of the disobedient one.

 "The older brother became angry and refused to go in [to the celebration]. So his father went out and pleaded with him. But he answered his father, 'Look! All these years I've been slaving for you and never disobeyed your orders. Yet you never gave me even a young goat so I could celebrate with my friends. But when this son of yours who has squandered your property with prostitutes comes home, you kill the fattened calf for him!'"

My guess is that this parable exposed their true motives for ostracizing the sinners among them. They worked hard to keep the Law and took pride in doing a good job. Those who didn't were being disobedient and deserved to be punished. By shunning them, the Pharisees were actually helping the Lord mete out the punishment. This made them feel all the better about themselves. Nothing like being on the Lord's side to make one feel righteous.

Then comes this itinerant preacher giving these sinners all kinds of attention and actually making them feel good about themselves, giving them hope, and taking away their motivation to clean up their act. It wasn't fair. The Pharisees worked so hard at being good and these sinners get all the attention. On top of that, the Pharisees labored to earn their ticket to eternity. If the sinners got a free pass, like Jesus seemed to be implying, what kind of example would that set? They were plainly jealous.

And so the Lord softened the blow with the last point in the parable. He had the joyful father say, "My son, you are always with me, and everything I have is yours. But we had to celebrate and be glad, because this brother of yours was dead and is alive again; he was lost and is found."

Rewarding sinners doesn't penalize the righteous. The Lord doesn't subscribe to the scarcity mentality, that there's only so much to go around and giving to one means taking from another. For everyone who asks will receive, all who seek will find, and to all who knock the door will be opened (**Matthew 7:7-8**).

AND FINALLY ...

It's easy to spot the Pharisees' error. They thought salvation was something they could earn, and by attempting to do so, they developed a self-righteous attitude that actually placed them further in their debt of sin. The only difference between the Pharisees and the sinners is that the sinners knew they needed a Savior. But the Lord's compassion for them, as expressed by the father in the parable to the older son, must have worked. On the Day of Pentecost, the newborn Church picked up over 3,000 members, many of them Pharisees and Teachers of the Law.

The Pharisees were a group from Biblical times, but they're not all dead yet. There's still plenty of that self-righteous "holier than thou" attitude around, and most of us harbor some of it. So next time you feel a little jealous when some undeserving sinner repents and is saved, remember, this brother of yours was dead and is alive again; he was lost and is found. And in Heaven, the angels rejoice.

BUT WAIT, THERE'S MORE

There's one more interpretation of this parable that bears a closer look. And that's to see the older son as the Gentile Church and the younger one as Israel, with God, of course, as the Father. And lest you think the order of the sons is backward, remember that technically the world was all Gentile till the time of Abraham, so it makes sense to see Israel as the younger son.

In this symbolic view, Israel departed from the covenant relationship to squander their inheritance in the world and for years was presumed dead. As the End of the Age approaches, Israel will return, signs of which we already see. But even in these early stages of return, we also see the jealousy of the older brother manifesting itself in parts of the Gentile Church. Having built their doctrines around "Replacement Theology" (believing that the Church has replaced Israel in God's view), they feel the Church has inherited the promises of Israel. Therefore, there's no purpose to be served by Israel's reappearance as a nation. The Church now serves as God's agency on Earth and will inherit the Kingdom.

But God says, "Only if the Heavens above can be measured and the foundations of the Earth below be searched out will I reject all the descendants of Israel because of all they have done." (**Jeremiah 31:27**) And in **Acts 15**, He had James tell us that after the Lord had taken a people for Himself from among the Gentiles, He would return to build David's fallen tabernacle.

The Lord speaks to the Gentile Church as the father spoke to his elder son. "My son, you are always with me, and everything I have is yours. But we had to celebrate and be glad, because this brother of yours was dead and is alive again; he was lost and is found."

Now you know the adult version.

CHAPTER FORTY-THREE

THE DEAD GIRL AND THE SICK WOMAN

A VIEW OF ISRAEL AND THE CHURCH

Jesus was answering a question posed to Him by disciples of John the Baptist:

> "How is it that we fast, and the Pharisees fast, but your disciples don't?" Jesus answered, "How can the guests of the Bridegroom mourn while he is with them? The time will come when the Bridegroom will be taken from them, and then they will fast." (**Matthew 9:14-15**)

> While he was saying this, a ruler came and knelt before him and said, "My daughter is dying. But come and put your hand on her, and she will live." Jesus got up and went with him, and so did his disciples.
>
> Just then a woman who had been subject to bleeding for twelve years came up behind him and touched the

edge of his cloak. She said to herself, "If I only touch his cloak, I will be healed."

Jesus turned and saw her. "Take heart, daughter," he said, "your faith has healed you." And the woman was healed from that moment.

When Jesus entered the ruler's house and saw the flute players and the noisy crowd, he said, "Go away. The girl is not dead but asleep." But they laughed at him. After the crowd had been put outside, he went in and took the girl by the hand, and she got up. News of this spread through all that region. (**Matthew 9:18-26**)

Matthew's account of this double miracle is an abbreviated one. It's also described in **Mark 5:22-43** and **Luke 8:47-56** where more detail is included. For example, we know from comparing the three passages that the ruler's name was Jairus and his dying daughter was 12 years old, born the same year that the woman contracted the bleeding problem. I'll add more details as we go along.

WHO'S WHO?

Jairus was Jewish, an official in a synagogue, and though her background isn't mentioned, the diseased woman must have been a Gentile, because a Jewish woman with an issue of blood would have been quarantined, not permitted among the people. Any Jew touching her would become ceremonially unclean, and so any time she was among other people, she would have had to cry out "Unclean!" to warn them away (**Leviticus 15:25-31**). As a Gentile she would have come under no such restriction and so was able to push her way through the crowd around Jesus (see **Mark 5:31**) to touch the hem of His garment.

While on His way to tend to the sick girl, Jesus felt the woman touch Him. Incidentally, the hem of a rabbi's garment contained special markings identifying his position or rank, similar to the chevrons on a soldier's arm. By touching the hem of the Lord's garment, the woman was appealing to His authority. As the Lord turned to confirm that her faith had healed her, He and Jairus were informed that the young daughter had died. Jesus told Jairus to pay no attention, commanding him, in effect, to believe the impossible (**Mark 5:36**).

Arriving at Jairus' home, the Lord drove the hired professional mourners away. He was now alone with the girl, her parents, and a few disciples. He commanded the girl to awaken, told her parents to get her some food, (proving she was not a spirit but had come back to life in the flesh), and admonished them to keep the miracle to themselves.

THE DEEPER MEANING

This miracle symbolizes the Mission of the Messiah during the Church Age in a most dramatic way. If we see the Jewish girl as Israel and the woman as the Gentiles it all becomes clear.

While Israel was alive and thriving, the Gentiles were dying, their sin nature like an incurable disease of the blood that slowly robbed them of their lives. This explains one significance of the number 12 in both their lives. In rejecting the Messiah, Israel died, and the offer of salvation was extended to all the Gentiles who diligently sought Him. (The Greek word translated **healed** in the passage also means *saved*.) Having saved them by their faith, the Messiah will turn again to Israel, raising her from spiritual death.

This symbolic interpretation is not mere speculation. It dovetails nicely with the prophecy quoted by James at the Council of Jerusalem. The topic of discussion was whether the door to salvation had been opened to the Gentiles.

 Simon has described to us how God first intervened to choose a people for his name from the Gentiles. The words of the prophets are in agreement with this, as it is written:

"After this I will return and rebuild David's fallen tent. Its ruins I will rebuild, and I will restore it, that the rest of mankind may seek the Lord, even all the Gentiles who bear my name, says the Lord, who does these things—things known from long ago." **(Acts 15:14-18)**

And it brings us to the other significance of the number 12. It's the number of governmental authority, emphasizing the fact that the Messiah has authority on Earth to heal the sick, raise the dead, and save the lost.

Now you know the adult version.

CHAPTER FORTY-FOUR

THE WORKERS IN THE VINEYARD

IT'S NOT WHAT YOU DO, IT'S WHO YOU KNOW

> For the kingdom of heaven is like a landowner who went out early in the morning to hire men to work in his vineyard. He agreed to pay them a denarius for the day and sent them into his vineyard. About the third hour he went out and saw others standing in the marketplace doing nothing. He told them, "You also go and work in my vineyard, and I will pay you whatever is right." So they went. He went out again about the sixth hour and the ninth hour and did the same thing. About the eleventh hour he went out and found still others standing around. He asked them, "Why have you been standing here all day long doing nothing?" "Because no one has hired us," they answered. He said to them, "You also go and work in my vineyard."

When evening came, the owner of the vineyard said to his foreman, "Call the workers and pay them their wages, beginning with the last ones hired and going on to the first." The workers who were hired about the eleventh hour came and each received a denarius. So when those came who were hired first, they expected to receive more. But each one of them also received a denarius. When they received it, they began to grumble against the landowner. "These men who were hired last worked only one hour," they said, "and you have made them equal to us who have borne the burden of the work and the heat of the day." But he answered one of them, "Friend, I am not being unfair to you. Didn't you agree to work for a denarius? Take your pay and go. I want to give the man who was hired last the same as I gave you. Don't I have the right to do what I want with my own money? Or are you envious because I am generous?" So the last will be first, and the first will be last. (**Matthew 20:1-16**)

WHAT GOOD THING MUST I DO?

This parable is given as the conclusion of a discussion that began a chapter earlier with a rich young man asking what good thing he must do to inherit eternal life (**Matthew 19:16-30**). By the way, some believe this young man was Mark, future Gospel writer, and companion of Paul. As you know, a parable is a Heavenly story set in an Earthly context. Everyone and everything is symbolic. The key to unlocking a parable is to interpret the symbolism correctly. Here's my view.

The vineyard represents the body of believers, and the landowner is the Lord. The workers are those from among the human race who respond to His call, the day is their lifetime, and the wages represent eternal life. All through our lives, God is calling. Some respond early in life, some later and others at the very end. But all who respond receive eternal life. For it is by grace you have been saved through faith, not by works (**Ephesians 2:8-9**).

Some workers in the parable resented the fact that all were paid equally, believing that since they worked longer, they should have received more. This attitude reflects the spiritual pride found in some long-term believers who think their years of service should automatically count for more. It actually betrays their works based theology, showing that they've forgotten that we serve the Lord to express our gratitude for what He's already done, not to earn more of what we expect Him to do. We should be grateful for long years of service because it means we've had more opportunities to say thanks. The landowner responded to these malcontents by saying that they had received everything he'd promised them. If he wanted to be generous with the others wasn't that His right?

 For my thoughts are not your thoughts, neither are your ways my ways," declares the Lord. (**Isaiah 55:8**)

Here on Earth, an employer who paid his people that way would be considered unfair and could be in violation of wage and hour laws. Compensation is normally based on performance and length of service. That was also the attitude of the rich young man who had asked, "What good thing must I do?" All his life he had been taught the relationship between effort and reward, and he wanted to know what he could do to earn his salvation.

But the Lord looks at things differently. His love for us is derived from who we are, not what we've done. And who are we? We are children of the King, the highest example of His creative capability, His work of art (**Romans 8:17 & Ephesians 2:10**). We don't have to work to earn eternal life, we just have to accept when He offers it. It's our inheritance, after all.

RICHES AND RIGHTEOUSNESS

The Israelites had been taught that riches were an indication of righteousness and when Jesus now told His disciples that it's hard for a rich man to enter the Kingdom, they asked, "Who then can be saved?" "With man this is impossible," Jesus replied, "But with God all things are possible" (**Matthew 19:23-26**). Still not willing to abandon their works theology Peter said, "We have left everything to follow you. What then will there be for us?" (**vs. 27**)

Then the Lord illustrated the distinction between the free gift of salvation and the rewards that come from properly motivated service. They would sit in judgment of the 12 tribes of Israel. Indeed everyone who has abandoned the things of this world in favor of a life of service would receive similar rewards, plus eternal life (**vs. 28-29**). Many who perceive themselves as deserving of superior rewards based solely on their hard work or length of service will discover that the Lord's criteria for such rewards is far different from their own. They will learn the meaning of His phrase, "the last will be first, and the first will be last." (**vs. 30**) It's the motive of our heart while serving Him that matters, not the duration or outcome of our effort (**1 Corinthians 3:10-15**). Their pride will have disqualified them for special rewards.

So the Parable of the Workers in the Vineyard teaches that no matter when in your life you heed His call, you will gain Eternal Life. It's a gift freely given to all who will receive it, irrespective of merit or effort. The only problem is that you can't determine in advance when your last chance to accept will come. Better make sure you've got it now.

Now you know the adult version.

CHAPTER FORTY-FIVE

TWO SONS AND A FEW TENANTS

WHO OWNS THIS PLACE?

It was one of those edgy discussions between the Priests and the Lord. They were questioning His authority again, and since they were unwilling to answer His question about the origin of John's baptism, He refused to answer their question about His authority.

Then He told them these two parables.

THE PARABLE OF THE TWO SONS

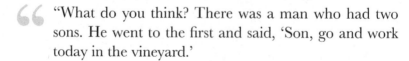

> "What do you think? There was a man who had two sons. He went to the first and said, 'Son, go and work today in the vineyard.'
>
> "'I will not,' he answered, but later he changed his mind and went.
>
> "Then the father went to the other son and said the same thing. He answered, 'I will, sir,' but he did not go.

"Which of the two did what his father wanted?"

"The first," they answered.

Jesus said to them, "Truly I tell you, the tax collectors and the prostitutes are entering the kingdom of God ahead of you. For John came to you to show you the way of righteousness, and you did not believe him, but the tax collectors and the prostitutes did. And even after you saw this, you did not repent and believe him. (**Matthew 21:28-32**)

THE PARABLE OF THE TENANTS

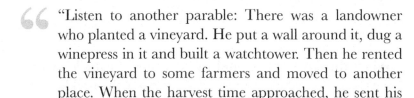

"Listen to another parable: There was a landowner who planted a vineyard. He put a wall around it, dug a winepress in it and built a watchtower. Then he rented the vineyard to some farmers and moved to another place. When the harvest time approached, he sent his servants to the tenants to collect his fruit.

"The tenants seized his servants; they beat one, killed another, and stoned a third. Then he sent other servants to them, more than the first time, and the tenants treated them the same way. Last of all, he sent his son to them. 'They will respect my son,' he said.

"But when the tenants saw the son, they said to each other, 'This is the heir. Come, let's kill him and take his inheritance.' So they took him and threw him out of the vineyard and killed him.

"Therefore, when the owner of the vineyard comes, what will he do to those tenants?"

"He will bring those wretches to a wretched end," they replied, "and he will rent the vineyard to other tenants, who will give him his share of the crop at harvest time."

Jesus said to them, "Have you never read in the Scriptures:

"'The stone the builders rejected

has become the cornerstone;

the Lord has done this,

and it is marvelous in our eyes'?

"Therefore I tell you that the kingdom of God will be taken away from you and given to a people who will produce its fruit. Anyone who falls on this stone will be broken to pieces; anyone on whom it falls will be crushed."

When the chief priests and the Pharisees heard Jesus' parables, they knew he was talking about them. They looked for a way to arrest him, but they were afraid of the crowd because the people held that he was a prophet. (**Matthew 21:33-46**)

I THINK THEY'VE GOT IT

These two parables are so obvious in their meaning, it's no wonder they got it. John's Baptism was one of repentance. By the way, let's correct the definition of that word. **Repent** means *to change your opinion about your behavior*, not *change your behavior*. When John said, "Repent for the Kingdom of Heaven is near," he wasn't warning people to clean up their act so they'd be qualified for the Kingdom. He knew that was impossible. He was telling them to change their opinion about needing a Savior before it was too late. His water baptism was a ceremonial cleansing from their sins, symbolizing salvation by faith following a confession of their need for a Savior.

The Lord's point was that those who realized their hopeless condition and received their cleansing by faith would enter the Kingdom ahead of those who felt no need for a cleansing and relied on their behavior instead. Way ahead.

The Pharisees worked hard to maintain the outward appearance of keeping the Law but failed miserably in their hearts, with their pride and feelings of superiority. The "sinners" on the other hand admitted they hadn't been able to please God with their behavior and came in faith alone with broken and contrite hearts. The Lord's preference for that attitude had been documented in their Scriptures for nearly 1,000 years (**Psalm 51:16-17**).

THE PARABLE OF THE TENANTS

As for the Parable of the Tenants, only the naming of names could have made this a clearer summary of their history. The Landowner was the Lord, the vineyard His Kingdom on Earth, the workers were the Israelites, His servants represented the prophets He regularly sent to Israel, and of course His son was Jesus. And when they answered the question about what should be done, they gave as pure a prophetic utterance as has ever come from the mouths of men. "He will bring those wretches to a wretched end," they replied, "and he will rent the vineyard to other tenants, who will give him his share of the crop at harvest time."

The Lord agreed. "Therefore I tell you that the kingdom of God will be taken away from you and given to a people who will produce its fruit. He who falls on this stone will be broken to pieces, but he on whom it falls will be crushed."

Here then are the only two options available. Fall on the stone (the Stone the builders rejected) and be broken, be humble and contrite, be born again and live by faith. Or keep going your own way till someday when you least expect it the Stone falls on you, and be called to account for your behavior, be crushed and die in your sins.

SO WHAT'S THE BIG MYSTERY HERE?

They knew He was talking about them, yet their response was contention, not contrition. Their hearts had become so hardened, they could no longer consider the possibility they might be mistaken. They had to shut Him up because they couldn't risk having to re-think things.

Back then, they had people who disagreed with them arrested. (Today we're much more subtle, we just re-interpret the meaning of what He said.) But they understood that He was threatening to take the Kingdom away from them and give it to others who would produce its fruit.

Now don't let anyone try to tell you that the vineyard is the Land of Israel. The land was given to them unconditionally. But beyond that, Israel was chosen by God to accomplish four things: to transmit His word (**Isaiah 42:9**), be a witness for Him (**Isaiah 43:10**), show forth His blessing (**Isaiah 49:3**) and be the channel for the Messiah (**Isaiah 49:5**).

They did such a remarkable job in transmitting His word that today hardly any of the Old Testament varies from the way God originally spoke it. And as a showcase for His blessing, the reigns of David and Solomon were unparalleled in previewing life in the Kingdom. Of course, it goes without saying that Israel was the channel for the Messiah. It was in the second area, being a witness for God, where they had failed.

 "Woe to you, teachers of the law and Pharisees, you hypocrites! You travel over land and sea to win a single convert, and when he becomes one, you make him twice as much a son of hell as you are," Jesus accused them. (**Matthew 23:15**)

On the Temple Mount, the Court of the Gentiles was as close as non-Jews could get to the Holy of Holies, and was the only place they could legally worship the Lord. Any attempt to get closer was a crime punishable by death. At the time of Jesus, it had been turned into an open-air market (it's the place from which Jesus drove the money-changers and sellers of animals) making it impossible for Gentiles to worship there. In short, the Lord promised He would be their God, but Israel had refused to share Him with anyone else.

GO YE INTO ALL THE WORLD

And so the Great Commission was given to the disciples and through them the Church. "All authority in Heaven and on Earth has been given to me," Jesus told them. "Therefore go and make disciples of all nations, baptizing them in the name of the Father and of the Son and of the Holy Spirit, and teaching them to obey everything I have commanded you. And surely I am with you always, to the very end of the age." (**Matthew 28:18-20**) Pretty soon now, we'll find out if we've done any better.

Now you know the adult version.

CHAPTER FORTY-SIX

THE GOOD SAMARITAN

WHO IS MY NEIGHBOR?

> On one occasion an expert in the Law stood up to test Jesus. "Teacher," he asked, "What must I do to inherit eternal life?" "What is written in the Law," Jesus replied, "How do you read it?" He answered: "Love the Lord your God with all your heart and with all your soul and with all your strength and with all your mind [Deuteronomy 6:5] and love your neighbor as yourself [Leviticus 19:18]." "You have answered correctly," Jesus replied, "Do this and you will live." But he wanted to justify himself and so he asked Jesus, "And who is my neighbor?" (**Luke 10:25-29**)

In reply, Jesus told the Parable of the Good Samaritan (**Luke 10:30-37**) the obvious point of which is that our neighbor is anyone in need of our assistance. But remember, parables are Heavenly stories put into an earthly context where every character is symbolic of someone or something else. The Parable of the Good Samaritan is no exception. Therefore we would expect to find a glimpse of Heaven contained within. As we've covered before, the word **parable** literally means *to place alongside*, so the obvious story has to be accompanied by another less obvious one. Let's find it.

WHO ARE THE SAMARITANS?

The Samaritans are the descendants of apostate Jews from the Northern Kingdom and pagans who had come to the region after Assyria conquered it in 721 BC. The Jews despised them because of their intermarriage and because they had incorporated pagan rituals into their worship of God (Jewish law forbade both). A generation or so before the time of Jesus, a son of the Jewish High Priest had run away and married the daughter of the King of Samaria, built a temple there and promoted a rival worship system which caused a massive scandal. In her encounter with Jesus (**John 4:4-42**) the Samaritan "woman at the well" makes reference to this (**verse 19**).

The region called Samaria was named after the capital city of the former Northern Kingdom and is located in what's known today as the West Bank. Because their laws prohibit marrying outside their own, the Samaritan population has dwindled to a point where only about 700 exist today. They're not Palestinians, but they're not regarded as Jews either and keep pretty much to themselves. Some have equated the Jews' treatment of Samaritans during the time of Jesus with the southern whites' treatment of blacks in the early part of the 20th century in the United States, so to have a Samaritan as the hero of this story must have gotten their attention right away. By the way, the ruins of the Samaritan Temple have been discovered and are being excavated for future public display.

AND NOW, BACK TO OUR STORY

You know the obvious part: A man traveling along the old Jericho Road is beset by robbers who strip him of his clothes, beat him, and leave him half dead. First a priest, and then a Levite pass by, but simply cross to the other side and ignore him. Then a Samaritan comes along. He comes to where the man is, binds up his wounds, applying oil and wine, and places him upon his own donkey. He takes the man to a nearby inn and cares for him. The next day he pays the man's present and future bill asking the innkeeper to look after him and promising to pay any balance due when he returns. The two silver coins he gave the innkeeper would have paid a man's hotel bill for up to two months in those days.

Understanding that there's supposed to be a glimpse of Heaven here and that everyone in the parable is symbolic, let's look for the hidden meaning. If we let the man represent you and me, we can easily discover who it is that would attack us, strip us of our clothing and leave us for dead. We know that our spiritual covering is often referred to in terms of clothing. "All our righteous works are as filthy rags," says **Isaiah 64:6** whereas the Lord clothes us with *garments of salvation* and *robes of righteousness* (**Isaiah 61:10**). And in **Revelation 19:8** our fine linen garments stand for *the righteous acts of the saints*. So who would strip us of our covering of righteousness and leave us spiritually dead? Only Satan—the stealer of our soul. The priest and the Levite represent organized religion that in and of itself is powerless to restore spiritual life and leaves us just as dead as when it found us.

WILL THE REAL GOOD SAMARITAN PLEASE STAND UP?

And that leaves the Good Samaritan. Though despised by His countrymen, He comes to where we are after we've been attacked and beaten by our enemy, stripped of all our righteousness and left hopelessly lost in our sins, beyond the ability of all our religious works to restore us to God's favor. He binds up our wounds, pours on oil (the Holy Spirit) and wine (the joy of our salvation) and carries us to a place of spiritual comfort where He personally cares for us. Upon leaving this earth He paid all the present and future debt created by our sins, (silver was the coin of redemption) promising to settle any remaining balance (perfecting us) when He returns. This could only be the Lord Jesus, without Whom no amount of religious work will suffice to protect us from our enemy, but Who has come to bind up the brokenhearted and proclaim freedom for the captives of sin (**Isaiah 61:1-2**). He is our refuge and strength, an ever-present help in times of trouble (**Psalm 46:1**).

Now you know the adult version.

CHAPTER FORTY-SEVEN

THE RICH MAN AND LAZARUS

AND THE FIRST WILL BE LAST

The story of the Rich Man and Lazarus is found only in the Gospel According to Luke (**16:19-31**) and is the clearest picture anywhere in Scripture of the afterlife. As such, it is essential reading for anyone attempting to counter the plethora of "life after death" accounts in secular and new age writings, as well as the notion of reincarnation found in some cults and Eastern religions.

The concept of life after death originates in Judaism. Job was the earliest to mention it (**Job 19:25-27**). But David, Isaiah, Daniel, and others, also wrote about the life that comes after death as a reward for righteousness. Daniel was the first to clarify that the unrighteous will also rise from the grave, and it's from his explanation (**Daniel 12:2**) that we've come to understand that everyone ever born lives forever. (Bodies are killed or wear out and expire, but spirits, the repositories of life, are eternal.) An angel explained to Daniel that while all rise from the grave, for some the second life brings everlasting reward, and for others everlasting shame and contempt. In **Revelation 20**, we learn that for the unsaved, their return from the grave is for judgment of their behavior while living. John wrote there about the second death—actually a conscious state of eternal and solitary separation from God accompanied by never ending torment—as the outcome of this judgment. Christians think of this as "hell," but as we'll learn from the Rich Man and Lazarus, it's really much worse.

WHAT'S THE STORY?

Here's a summary: A rich man lived in the lap of luxury, while a beggar (Lazarus) languished outside his gate hoping for table scraps. In due time, they both died. Angels carried Lazarus to "Abraham's side (bosom)" a popular Jewish term in that day for the abode of the dead, also called Paradise. Jesus promised one of the men being crucified with Him that they would meet there before the end of the day. The Hebrew name for this place is Sheol, while the Greeks called it Hades from which the English word Hell is derived. The rich man also went there upon dying, but while Lazarus was being comforted, the rich man was in constant torment. Asking Abraham for relief, he was informed that while they were within sight and speaking distance of each other, they were actually in two different areas and there was no way to cross from one to the other (**Luke 16:19-26**).

The rich man then asked Abraham to send Lazarus back to warn his brothers, still alive, to change their opinion about the need for a Savior so as to avoid coming there. Abraham refused, saying, "They have Moses and the Prophets (now books in our Old Testament), let them listen to them." "No", said the rich man, "But if someone from the dead goes to them, they will repent." Abraham responded, "If they will not listen to Moses and the Prophets, they will not be convinced even if someone rises from the dead." (**Luke 16:27-31**)

WHAT'S THE POINT?

There are three points actually:

1. The only place to secure your eternal destiny is here on earth

before you die. The rich man never asked for a second chance for himself, only that his brothers be warned while they were still living to avoid sharing his fate. Having experienced the alternative, there's no way he would turn down an opportunity to join Abraham and Lazarus if one existed for him. Abraham made it clear that it was impossible to cross from either area to the other.

2. The Bible contains all the facts you need to make an informed decision about eternity and is the Lord's chosen method for bringing His children to Salvation.

3. When folks aren't convinced by Scripture, even someone coming back from the dead will fail to persuade them, a fact the Lord Himself proved all too convincingly a few weeks later.

GRACE THROUGH FAITH

Before the cross, those who had died in faith of a coming Savior, as the Scriptures taught them, went to a temporary place of comfort to rest until, in the fullness of time, their Redeemer's shed blood finally erased the penalty for their sins. This is Paradise, the place called Abraham's bosom in the passage.

When Jesus came to Sheol after His death on the cross, He commended them for their faith (**1 Peter 4:6**) and took them to Heaven (**Matthew 27:52-53**). His crucifixion removed the final obstacle to their entry into God's presence. All who have died in faith since the cross go straight into the Lord's presence (**2 Corinthians 5:7-8**) where they await reunion with their resurrection bodies (**1 Thessalonians 4:16**). They are the only group of believers more anxious for the Rapture of the Church than we are (**Romans 8:18-23**).

The unsaved dead will continue to languish with the rich man until the end of the Millennium when they too are raised, judged, and then banished to a place of eternal torment, but this time in utter separation and darkness (**Revelation 20:15**).

Many in the liberal church, in cults, the New Age, and in the Eastern religions speak of another chance to reconcile with God following physical death. Some even promote reincarnation into a series of lives through which people work their way toward perfection, eventually earning their place with God or even becoming a god. The Bible speaks of no such things, teaching instead, that "man is destined to die once and after that to face judgment." (**Hebrews 9:27**) The Lord's own words in the story of the Rich Man and Lazarus confirm this.

TRICK OR TREAT?

What a great trick of our enemy, persuading supposedly learned theologians to teach their Biblically ignorant followers to ignore the clear admonitions of Scripture and seek an alternate way—only to discover after it's too late that they were misled. For wide is the gate and broad is the road that leads to destruction and many enter through it. But small is the gate and narrow the road that leads to life, and only a few find it (**Matthew 7:13-14**). In the context of these two verses, all are seeking the path to salvation, but only a few find it. Most choose the complex over the simple, the wide over the small, the broad over the narrow.

Here's the simple, small and narrow truth. God, Who created us, requires us to live by His law. Sin is the violation of God's law, and the penalty is death. Because you sin you can't avoid the penalty, but because He loves you so much Jesus offered to die in your place. God agreed to this and has issued you a full pardon. You need only to ask to be forgiven of all your sins, past, present, and future and receive your pardon. When you do, your eternal destiny changes from torment to Paradise, from separation to union, from death to life. Period. End of story.

Now you know the adult version.

CHAPTER FORTY-EIGHT

THE WEDDING BANQUET

WHERE'S THE BRIDE?

> Jesus spoke to them again in parables, saying: "The kingdom of heaven is like a king who prepared a wedding banquet for his son. He sent his servants to those who had been invited to the banquet to tell them to come, but they refused to come.
>
> "Then he sent some more servants and said, 'Tell those who have been invited that I have prepared my dinner: My oxen and fattened cattle have been butchered, and everything is ready. Come to the wedding banquet.' But they paid no attention and went off—one to his field, another to his business. The rest seized his servants, mistreated them and killed them. The king was enraged. He sent his army and destroyed those murderers and burned their city.
>
> "Then he said to his servants, 'The wedding banquet is ready, but those I invited did not deserve to come. Go

to the street corners and invite to the banquet anyone you find.' So the servants went out into the streets and gathered all the people they could find, both good and bad, and the wedding hall was filled with guests.

"But when the king came in to see the guests, he noticed a man there who was not wearing wedding clothes. 'Friend,' he asked, 'how did you get in here without wedding clothes?' The man was speechless.

"Then the king told the attendants, 'Tie him hand and foot, and throw him outside, into the darkness, where there will be weeping and gnashing of teeth.'

"For many are invited, but few are chosen." **(Matthew 22:1-14)**

WHY ALL THE PARABLES?

When Jesus was asked why He spoke to the people in parables so often, He said in effect that there were two reasons: 1: to instruct His followers, and 2: to confuse everyone else.

The Parable of the Wedding Banquet is a good example. It's either instructive or confusing, depending on your knowledge and understanding of Jewish wedding customs during Biblical times.

Am I suggesting that ignorance of those customs disqualifies us as followers of Jesus? No, but I am convinced that acquiring a literal, historical, and grammatical understanding of Scripture will bring you closer to the Lord than almost anything else you can do.

Literal means we believe the Bible is the inspired word of God to be taken at face value unless there is compelling reason to do otherwise (usually indicated in the context of the passage).

Historical means that each passage is put into its proper historical setting, and surrounded with the thoughts, attitudes and feelings prevalent at the time of writing.

Grammatical means that words are given meanings consistent with their common understanding in the original language at the time of writing.

THE WEDDING PLANNER

First-century Jewish wedding customs held that the father of the groom was in charge of the event and bore all the expense associated with the wedding and reception. In the case of royalty or the wealthy, this often included providing a specially made garment to be worn over a guest's regular clothing. This wedding garment was presented to the guest upon arrival and donned immediately. Wearing it wasn't mandatory, but was considered a great insult to the father of the groom if refused. And, refusing the wedding garment could get a guest ejected from the festivities. In the case of large gatherings, it also served as identification to discourage uninvited guests from crashing the party.

The parables of our Lord Jesus are earthly stories meant to explain Heavenly truths. Each person or object is symbolic of someone or something else. Understanding the symbolism is crucial to discovering the lesson of the Parable. This is entirely consistent with literal, historical, grammatical interpretation since the passage is clearly described as a parable, and in fact gaining the theological impact of this parable requires such an understanding.

The King is God the Father, His Son our Lord Jesus. Invited guests represent Israel. And the servants He sent are the prophets. The city He destroyed, when His invited guests refused to attend and killed His servants, is Jerusalem.

DO YOU KNOW THE BRIDE?

Some say those He then sent His servants out to invite represent the Church, which does contain both good and bad, but the symbolism and timing are wrong. The Church is the Bride of Christ, not a group of last minute substitute guests. Since Israel had already refused their invitation, and the Church (being the bride) would not need an invitation, who could these guests be?

They have to come from a time after the Bride is chosen and prepared, the wedding banquet is ready and only the guests are lacking for the festivities to begin. Therefore, they have to be a group we call Tribulation Saints, those who come to faith after the Rapture of the Church in **Revelation 4**, but before the Wedding of the Lamb in **Revelation 19**. The servants He sends out to invite them are the 144,000 evangelists of **Revelation 7**, and the two witnesses of **Revelation 11**. These Tribulation Saints begin showing up in Heaven in **Revelation 7**, and more arrive in **Revelation 15**.

HERE'S THE REAL LESSON OF THE PARABLE

The wedding garment represents His righteousness—yet another Biblical reference to clothing as our spiritual covering. As stated earlier in the Parable of the Good Samaritan, Isaiah described our righteousness as filthy rags (**Isaiah 64:6**) and His as "garments of salvation" and "robes of righteousness" (**Isaiah 61:10**) where the acquisition of these qualities is likened to clothing given us at a wedding.

In **Revelation 19** the Church is seen prepared as a bride having been clothed in white linen, again representing righteousness. In both cases, the righteousness symbolized by the clothing is given us —not purchased or earned.

The fact that one is thrown out for not wearing wedding clothes indicates these last-minute guests have to be clothed in "garments of salvation" meaning they're believers. And it's important to note that the place into which the gate-crasher was thrown is the "outer darkness" the place of eternal separation from God, the final destination of unbelievers.

Many are invited, but few are chosen. He doesn't desire that any should perish, but that all would come to repentance (**2 Peter 3:9**).

But whether it's the Bride or the wedding guests, the only right-eousness that gains us admission into the presence of God is that which is given us as a gift and accepted in faith (**Romans 4:5**). All of you who were baptized into Christ have clothed yourselves with Christ (**Galatians 3:27**). For God made Him Who had no sin to be sin for us, that in Him we might become the righteousness of God (**2 Corinthians 5:21**).

Now you know the adult version.

CHAPTER FORTY-NINE

RAISING LAZARUS FROM THE DEAD

FROM DEAD AND DEFEATED TO DELIVERED AND DANGEROUS

Lazarus, the brother of Mary and Martha of Bethany, lay sick at the point of death. The sisters sent word to Jesus, who was several days journey away. Hearing of his illness, Jesus assured the disciples that Lazarus wouldn't die, that this had occurred so "God's Son may be glorified through it." **(John 11:4)**

Since He knew by then that Lazarus was already dead, **(John 11:14-15)** and since He also knew what He was going to do, Jesus delayed His departure so by the time He arrived in Bethany, Lazarus had been dead for four days **(John 11:17)**. In the Jewish culture of the day, it was believed that the spirit of a dead person lingered near the body for three days before departing. It was only then that decomposition of the body began. By day four everyone would know Lazarus was truly dead.

 "Lord," Martha said to Jesus, "if you had been here, my brother would not have died. But I know that even now God will give you whatever you ask."

Jesus said to her, "Your brother will rise again."

Martha answered, "I know he will rise again in the resurrection at the last day."

Jesus said to her, "I am the resurrection and the life. He who believes in me will live, even though he dies; and whoever lives and believes in me will never die. Do you believe this?"

"Yes, Lord," she told him, "I believe that you are the Christ, the Son of God, who was to come into the world." (**John 11:21-27**)

YOU COULD HAVE PREVENTED THIS

Martha was the more practical of the sisters, and always had clear expectations of others. Once, she asked Jesus to scold Mary for sitting around listening to Him while she prepared food for the people gathered there. Now she gently took the Lord to task for not arriving in time to heal Lazarus. Jesus responded by taking Martha's spiritual pulse. Did she really believe that even now Jesus could help?

Thinking He was comforting her by referring to the End Times resurrection spoken of by Daniel, Isaiah, and others, she agreed she would see her brother again at the last day. She didn't understand that He was trying to tell her she would see him again on that very day. But her confession of Jesus as the promised Messiah was enough to satisfy Him. After all, how many people had seen loved ones returned to them after four days in the grave?

 And after she had said this, she went back and called her sister Mary aside. "The Teacher is here," she said, "and is asking for you." When Mary heard this, she got up quickly and went to him. Now Jesus had not yet entered the village but was still at the place where Martha had met him. When the Jews, who had been with Mary in the house comforting her, noticed how quickly she got up and went out, they followed her, supposing she was going to the tomb to mourn there.

When Mary reached the place where Jesus was and saw him, she fell at his feet and said, "Lord, if you had been here, my brother would not have died."

When Jesus saw her weeping, and the Jews who had come along with her also weeping, he was deeply moved in spirit and troubled. "Where have you laid him?" he asked.

"Come and see, Lord," they replied.

Jesus wept. Then the Jews said, "See how he loved him!"

But some of them said, "Could not he who opened the eyes of the blind man have kept this man from dying?" **(John 11:28-37)**

Even Mary, the romantic idealist of the two sisters, could not have predicted what was about to happen, and her obvious emotion had an effect on everyone around her, as the mourners and even Jesus wept with her. But as it is today, so it was then. Looking to assign the blame for the death of Lazarus, some criticized the Lord's apparent lack of timely attention to his need.

JESUS RAISES LAZARUS FROM THE DEAD

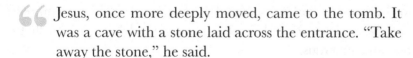

Jesus, once more deeply moved, came to the tomb. It was a cave with a stone laid across the entrance. "Take away the stone," he said.

"But, Lord," said Martha, the sister of the dead man, "by this time there is a bad odor, for he has been there four days."

Then Jesus said, "Did I not tell you that if you believed, you would see the glory of God?"

So they took away the stone. Then Jesus looked up and said, "Father, I thank you that you have heard me. I knew that you always hear me, but I said this for the benefit of the people standing here, that they may believe that you sent me."

When he had said this, Jesus called in a loud voice, "Lazarus, come out!" The dead man came out, his hands and feet wrapped with strips of linen, and a cloth around his face.

Jesus said to them, "Take off the grave clothes and let him go." **(John 11:38-44)**

So stunning was this miracle, that it accomplished the Lord's will in a way that nothing else could have. God's Son was glorified, and many who were there placed their faith in Him. But some, fearing this would continue a trend of belief in Jesus that would result in a complete overthrow of the nation, looked for a way to kill Lazarus (again) **(John 12:10)**.

More urgently, Jesus would have to die. In a remarkable demonstration of prophecy, Caiaphas the High Priest, exclaimed to the leadership, "You know nothing at all! You do not realize that it is better for you that one man die for the people than that the whole nation perish." **(John 11:49-50)** Of course, he was just speaking of killing Jesus to preserve the status quo, but no one could have more clearly explained the Lord's plan for the salvation of mankind.

As for Lazarus, he had now entered the final phase of his adventure. Having been defeated and dead, he was now delivered, and that made him dangerous.

In our last glimpse of this family, just before the last Passover He would spend on Earth, Jesus called on the home of Martha, Mary, and Lazarus. A dinner was held in His honor that gives us a beautiful picture of life in the Kingdom. Martha, representing the host of Heaven served the meal, while Lazarus, in the role of the Redeemed, reclined at the banquet table with the Lord.

And Mary, performing one of the purest and most intimate acts of worship to be found anywhere in Scripture, took the anointing perfume that had probably cost her a year's income and that she had been saving for her wedding night, and poured it over the Lord's feet. Letting down her hair, something a woman of her day would only do in the presence of her husband, she wiped His feet with it. And the whole house was filled with the fragrance of the perfume. What a model of The Bride of Christ.

Now you know the adult version.

CHAPTER FIFTY

PALM SUNDAY

BEHOLD YOUR KING

Jesus took the Twelve aside and told them, "We are going up to Jerusalem, and everything that is written by the prophets about the Son of Man will be fulfilled. He will be handed over to the Gentiles. They will mock him, insult him, spit on him, flog him and kill him. On the third day he will rise again." (**Luke 18:31-33**) They didn't understand what He was talking about, and He knew they wouldn't until afterward. They hadn't received the Holy Spirit yet, so it was supernaturally hidden from them.

Just before they reached Bethany, on the eastern slope of the Mount of Olives, He sent two of them ahead into the village to get a donkey for Him to ride. He said they'd find one that had never been ridden, tied to a tree there. He told them if anyone questioned them to say, "The Lord has need of it." They found everything just as He had described.

As He rode over the crest of the Mount of Olives toward Jerusalem, the crowd around Him broke into spontaneous praise, singing Psalms written for the entrance of the King into the Holy City. By tradition, they were held in reserve for the coming of the Messiah. Waving palm branches, and spreading their cloaks on the ground before Him, the crowd around Jesus must have created quite a spectacle, taking the breath away from most of those present.

But not all of them.

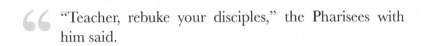

> "Teacher, rebuke your disciples," the Pharisees with him said.

In the view of the Pharisees, the crowd was committing blasphemy by suggesting Jesus was the Messiah King.

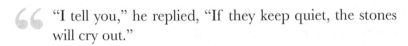

> "I tell you," he replied, "If they keep quiet, the stones will cry out."
>
> As he approached Jerusalem and saw the city, he wept over it and said, "If you, even you, had only known on this day what would bring you peace—but now it is hidden from your eyes. The days will come upon you when your enemies will build an embankment against you and encircle you and hem you in from every side. They will dash you to the ground, you and the children within your walls. They will not leave one stone upon another because you did not recognize the time of God's coming to you." (**Luke 19:39-44**)

WHAT DAY IS THIS?

The prophet Daniel had laid out the schedule for the Jews 500 years earlier. From the time they were freed from Babylon and given permission to rebuild Jerusalem, (it had been destroyed 70 years earlier) to the coming of the Messiah there would be 69 periods of 7 years each, or 483 years (**Daniel 9:25**). History tells us that the Persian ruler Artaxerxes Longimonus gave the needed permission in March of 445 BC (**Nehemiah 2:1-9**). The Sunday when Jesus rode a donkey into Jerusalem to the shouts of **Psalm 118:25-26** was exactly 483 years later, but by then most of the Jewish leadership no longer took the Bible literally, and the validity of predictive prophecy was being denied. In short, they missed the day's significance entirely.

The Lord, however, held them accountable for knowing when He would visit. They might not have known the day or hour but should have "recognized the time of God's coming." With over 300 clear prophecies being fulfilled in their midst, we can see His point. Remember, all 300 were fulfilled in the span of one generation, the one in which He came. And this particular day had been appointed in history for over 500 years. That's why, when the Pharisees advised Jesus to rebuke His followers for calling Him the Messiah, Jesus said, "I tell you, if they keep quiet, the stones will cry out." (**Luke 19:40**) (Don't you wish everyone had kept still for a minute or two?)

Of the other prophecies being fulfilled that day, one of the most remarkable is contained in the ritual of Passover. Remember, John had introduced Jesus to Israel by saying, "Look, the Lamb of God, Who takes away the sin of the world." (**John 1:29**) Here was a clear reference to Passover, where on the 10th day of the first month a lamb was set aside to be carefully inspected until the 14th to make sure it was qualified to be the sacrifice. It had to be a male without spot or blemish. Being found worthy, it was slain on the 14th.

On Palm Sunday, Jesus presented Himself publicly as King of Israel for the only time in His life. In doing so, He was offering Himself as the Passover Lamb. In Israel, it was the 10th day of the first month, and for the next three days He would be subjected to the most intense public scrutiny of His entire ministry. The Scribes and Pharisees were probing desperately to find some flaw in His teaching, figuratively looking for a spot or blemish that would disqualify Him. After three days, they finally gave up, unable to detect any imperfection. And as **Matthew 22:46** declares, "From that day on, no one dared to ask Him any more questions." The next day was the 14th, called Preparation Day in the Lord's time, and having been found worthy, He was crucified.

NOW WHAT?

There are over 500 prophecies relating to His Second Coming, and again, all will be fulfilled within the span of one generation (**Matthew 24:34**). Just as before, the fulfillment of these prophecies began when Jerusalem became a Jewish city again in 1967 (**Luke 21:24**), and just as before, our leaders no longer take the Bible literally, and the validity of predictive prophecy is being denied. But just as before, the Lord holds us accountable to "recognize the time of God's coming."

Israel was looking for the Lion of the Tribe of Judah to throw off the Roman yoke and restore Israel's kingdom. When they got the Lamb of God, who takes away the sin of the world, they weren't prepared and didn't recognize Him. Because of the mainline Church's liberal theology, many in the world today are looking for the Lamb of God and will be totally unprepared when the Lion of the Tribe of Judah comes to defeat His enemies and restore God's Kingdom. Like Santayana said, "Those who cannot remember the past are condemned to repeat it."

Now you know the adult version.

CHAPTER FIFTY-ONE

THE HEALING AT THE POOL

DO YOU WANT TO GET WELL?

" Some time later, Jesus went up to Jerusalem for one of the Jewish festivals. Now there is in Jerusalem near the Sheep Gate a pool, which in Aramaic is called Bethesda and which is surrounded by five covered colonnades. Here a great number of disabled people used to lie—the blind, the lame, the paralyzed. One who was there had been an invalid for thirty-eight years. When Jesus saw him lying there and learned that he had been in this condition for a long time, he asked him, "Do you want to get well?"

"Sir," the invalid replied, "I have no one to help me into the pool when the water is stirred. While I am trying to get in, someone else goes down ahead of me."

Then Jesus said to him, "Get up! Pick up your mat and walk." At once the man was cured; he picked up his mat and walked.

The day on which this took place was a Sabbath, and so the Jews said to the man who had been healed, "It is the Sabbath; the law forbids you to carry your mat."

But he replied, "The man who made me well said to me, 'Pick up your mat and walk.'"

So they asked him, "Who is this fellow who told you to pick it up and walk?"

The man who was healed had no idea who it was, for Jesus had slipped away into the crowd that was there.

Later Jesus found him at the temple and said to him, "See, you are well again. Stop sinning or something worse may happen to you." The man went away and told the Jews that it was Jesus who had made him well. (**John 5:1-15**)

MERCY IN THE HOUSE OF MERCY

Here's a miracle fraught with symbolism, one of only seven included in John's Gospel. Bethesda means "House of Mercy" in English and gives us a clue that there's more going on than meets the eye. For example, many invalids were lying around the pool. Why did Jesus only heal this one? This was clearly not a demonstration of His healing power. We're supposed to look for a deeper meaning.

The crippled man had been so for 38 years, the same amount of time Israel wandered in the wilderness while the rebellious generation died off after refusing to cross over into the Promised Land (**Deuteronomy 2:14**). When Jesus asked him, "Do you want to get well?" The crippled Israelite gave a graphic example of the poverty of the Law.

According to tradition, an angel periodically came down to stir up the waters of the pool. The first one into the stirred-up water was healed. Being crippled, he couldn't get to the water in time to be healed, and if he had been able to, he wouldn't have needed heal-ing. Being infested with sin, we can't keep the Law well enough to be saved, and if we could, we wouldn't need to be saved. It's a catch 22.

FIND THE DEEPER MEANING

The cripple was a type of Israel, a people who needed salvation but whose means to achieve it was incapable of success. The Messiah came to them asking if they wanted to be saved, and although many all around them said yes, ultimately they didn't know who He was.

The fact that the healing took place on the Sabbath, as did many, and that the rulers objected, symbolizes their rejection of Him in favor of their incompetent traditions. When Jesus told the man to stop sinning, He was telling him to resist going back to the Law for his remedy, since the fulfillment of the Law had come. The some-thing worse that could happen to him would be the forfeiture of his soul because now the man knew it was Jesus Who had healed him.

The Law is only a shadow of the good things that are coming—not the realities themselves. For this reason, it can never, by the same sacrifices repeated endlessly year after year, make perfect those who draw near to worship. If the Law could, would the sacrifices not have stopped being offered? For the worshipers would have been cleansed once for all, and would no longer have felt guilty for their sins.

 Day after day every priest stands and performs his religious duties. Again and again, he offers the same sacrifices, which can never take away sins. But when this priest (Jesus) had offered for all time one sacrifice for sins (himself), he sat down at the right hand of God. Since that time, he waits for his enemies to be made his footstool because by one sacrifice he has made perfect forever those who are being made holy. **(Hebrews 10:1-2 & 11-14)**

Now you know the adult version.

CHAPTER FIFTY-TWO

CLEANSING THE TEMPLE

A HOUSE OF PRAYER OR A DEN OF THIEVES?

> When it was almost time for the Jewish Passover, Jesus went up to Jerusalem. In the temple courts he found men selling cattle, sheep and doves, and others sitting at tables exchanging money. So he made a whip out of cords, and drove all from the temple area, both sheep and cattle; he scattered the coins of the money changers and overturned their tables. To those who sold doves he said, "Get these out of here! How dare you turn my Father's house into a market!"

His disciples remembered that it is written: "Zeal for your house will consume me." [**Psalm 69:9**]

Then the Jews demanded of him, "What miraculous sign can you show us to prove your authority to do all this?"

Jesus answered them, "Destroy this temple, and I will raise it again in three days."

The Jews replied, "It has taken forty-six years to build this temple, and you are going to raise it in three days?" But the temple he had spoken of was his body. After he was raised from the dead, his disciples recalled what he had said. Then they believed the Scripture and the words that Jesus had spoken. (**John 2:13-22**)

WHEN DID THAT HAPPEN?

Let's clear up the controversy over the placement of this event first. As we see, John put it right near the beginning of his Gospel while Matthew, Mark, and Luke tell the story in conjunction with the events of the Monday following Palm Sunday, at the end of the Lord's ministry.

Chronologically, they're right. The problem exists because John didn't always place events in chronological order. He moved them around to suit his purpose—which was to portray Jesus as the Son of God. Changing water into wine, cleansing the Temple, and His conversation with Nicodemus were placed together at the beginning of his Gospel to make that claim right off the bat. Far from being a day-by-day journal of the Lord's ministry, John's Gospel is focused on only 21 days out of the three and a half years. He uses ten chapters to cover the Lord's last week, and more than one quarter of the 879 verses in John's Gospel describe one day.

Over the centuries, Jews had migrated to all parts of the known world, but the Law required them to present themselves before God at the Temple in Jerusalem at least three times each year, Passover, Pentecost, and Tabernacles. Even that was too difficult for some, but everyone came for Passover. Carrying animals for sacrifice as well as food and portable shelter for a long journey wasn't always practical, so many out-of-towners brought money and purchased what they needed when they got there.

While in Jerusalem, they also had to pay the annual Temple tax, and the priests required it be paid in a special silver coinage minted by only them, hence the need for money changers. Over the years the temptation to charge premium prices to a captive audience proved too great to ignore, and so by the time of Jesus exchange rates were abysmal and animal prices were exorbitant.

On top of that, there was only one place a Gentile could come and worship, and that was in the Court of the Gentiles. Signs on the various gates clearly stated that to venture into any other area was punishable by death. So when the open air markets and money changing booths expanded to fill most all the Court of the Gentiles, they were left with no place to worship.

RIGHTEOUS INDIGNATION

When Jesus saw what they had done, He became furious. "It is written," He said to them, "'My house will be called a house of prayer for all nations,' but you are making it a 'den of robbers.'" (**Mark 11:17**) This statement combined quotes from Isaiah and Jeremiah to condemn them for usurping the Gentiles' place of worship and overcharging the pilgrims. He then scattered the money changing tables and drove out the sellers of sacrificial animals.

The fact that no one harmed or arrested Him or even tried to stop Him defies human logic. They simply asked by what authority He did this, and what miraculous sign He would give to confirm it. (That alone shows they suspected He had supernatural authority.)

Think about it for a minute, especially if you've heard the silly notion that by now in His ministry, events had overtaken Jesus, and He had lost control of His own destiny. He had just single-handedly destroyed one of the most lucrative scams in the whole country, right under the noses of both the Temple authorities and the Roman soldiers, and not only did He live to tell about it, He simply walked through guards, the soldiers, and the astonished crowds and went home.

But He didn't ignore their question. "Destroy this Temple, and I will raise it again in three days," He answered. He was, of course, speaking about His death and resurrection, a miracle of epic proportion that they didn't understand till after it happened, if at all.

And then He healed the sick all along the route of His departure, while the children shouted, "Hosannah to the Son of David!" The leaders watched, indignant. It was only Monday. It wasn't going to be a good week.

Now you know the adult version.

CHAPTER FIFTY-THREE

THE BLIND BEGGAR

NONE SO BLIND AS THOSE WHO WILL NOT SEE

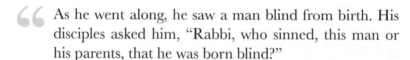

As he went along, he saw a man blind from birth. His disciples asked him, "Rabbi, who sinned, this man or his parents, that he was born blind?"

"Neither this man nor his parents sinned," said Jesus, "but this happened so that the work of God might be displayed in his life. As long as it is day, we must do the work of him who sent me. Night is coming, when no one can work. While I am in the world, I am the light of the world."

Having said this, he spit on the ground, made some mud with the saliva, and put it on the man's eyes. "Go," he told him, "wash in the Pool of Siloam" (this word means Sent). So the man went and washed, and came home seeing.

His neighbors and those who had formerly seen him

begging asked, "Isn't this the same man who used to sit and beg?" Some claimed that he was.

Others said, "No, he only looks like him."

But he himself insisted, "I am the man."

"How then were your eyes opened?" they demanded.

He replied, "The man they call Jesus made some mud and put it on my eyes. He told me to go to Siloam and wash. So I went and washed, and then I could see."

"Where is this man?" they asked him.

"I don't know," he said. (**John 9:1-12**)

Jesus came to offer Himself as Israel's Messiah and made every possible effort to demonstrate His power to them in fulfillment of their Scriptures. He healed them in the synagogues, on the Sabbath, in the Temple, always in public, and often in the presence of their leadership. In this case, which, like many, took place on the Sabbath, He didn't even wait for the blind man to ask Him for healing. This was a sovereign act of God, pure and simple, meant to convey a lesson.

Then He went out of His way to violate the prohibition against working on the Sabbath, making a mud paste out of saliva and dirt, and then spreading it on the man's eyes. (Since Jesus hadn't used that method before, there's no reason to believe that the mud was necessary for the healing.)

The subsequent discussions in verses 13-41 offer an excellent example of how preconceived notions can cause two different groups to draw opposite conclusions from the same event. The Pharisees, coming from the position that working on the Sabbath is wrong, concluded that Jesus was a sinner, while others, who started with the evidence of a miracle, believed He was sent by God. Some of the Pharisees said, "This man is not from God, for he does not keep the Sabbath." But others asked, "How can a sinner do such miraculous signs?" (**John 9:16**) Even the unimpeachable evidence presented by the beggar's ability to see was not enough for those who refused to believe.

"Nobody has ever heard of opening the eyes of a man born blind. If this man were not from God, he could do nothing," said the beggar. He was implying that healing a man who had lost his previously functioning eyesight was something special, but not unique. Giving sight to a man born blind had never been done before. The One who had done this had to be from God.

To this, they replied, "You were steeped in sin at birth; how dare you lecture us!" And they threw him out (**John 9:32-34**). They might have said, "Don't confuse us with facts, our minds are made up."

Then the Lord revealed the real lesson, for whom it was meant, and why He had gone out of His way to attract their attention.

Jesus heard that they had thrown him out, and when he found him, he said, "Do you believe in the Son of Man?"

"Who is he, sir?" the man asked. "Tell me so that I may believe in him."

Jesus said, "You have now seen him; in fact, he is the one speaking with you."

Then the man said, "Lord, I believe," and he worshiped him.

Jesus said, "For judgment I have come into this world, so that the blind will see and those who see will become blind."

Some Pharisees who were with him heard him say this and asked, "What? Are we blind too?"

Jesus said, "If you were blind, you would not be guilty

of sin; but now that you claim you can see, your guilt remains." (**John 9:35-41**)

The last obstacle to acquiring the truth is the belief that you already have it. Giving sight to the blind was a major Messianic sign in Old Testament prophecy, and Jesus performed this kind of miracle more often than any other.

But being so entrenched in their position, the Pharisees didn't recognize the Object of their worship even when He stood before them. The blind man, with no preconceived idea, fell to his knees and worshiped immediately upon being introduced.

Now you know the adult version.

CHAPTER FIFTY-FOUR

THE PARABLE OF THE TEN VIRGINS

WHERE IS THE BRIDE?

"At that time the kingdom of heaven will be like ten virgins who took their lamps and went out to meet the bridegroom. Five of them were foolish and five were wise. The foolish ones took their lamps but did not take any oil with them. The wise, however, took oil in jars along with their lamps. The bridegroom was a long time in coming, and they all became drowsy and fell asleep.

"At midnight the cry rang out: 'Here's the bridegroom! Come out to meet him!'

"Then all the virgins woke up and trimmed their lamps. The foolish ones said to the wise, 'Give us some of your oil; our lamps are going out.' 'No,' they replied, 'there may not be enough for both us and you. Instead, go to those who sell oil and buy some for yourselves.'

"But while they were on their way to buy the oil, the bridegroom arrived. The virgins who were ready went in with him to the wedding banquet. And the door was shut.

"Later the others also came. 'Sir! Sir!' they said. 'Open the door for us!' But he replied, 'I tell you the truth, I don't know you.'

"Therefore keep watch, because you do not know the day or the hour." (**Matthew 25:1-13**)

WHAT IS THAT ALL ABOUT?

Many incorrectly think this parable has to do with the Church, particularly, those who cling to the post-Tribulation Rapture viewpoint. Let's apply some standard rules of interpretation to see what it really means.

For the timing of the event, there's little debate since it's clearly disclosed. The opening phrase "At that time" refers to several earlier references in the Olivet Discourse all pointing to **Matthew 24:29** which says, "Immediately after the distress [Tribulation] of those days..."

This verse refers to the Great Tribulation, a three and a half year sequence of judgments. These judgments begin after the appearance of the "abomination that causes desolation, standing in the Holy Place," (commonly thought to be the antichrist, standing in the newly rebuilt Jewish Temple in Israel proclaiming himself to be god, as prophesied by Paul in **2 Thessalonians 2:4**).

So the timing of the parable is just after the end of the Great Tribulation when what's left of the world awaits the appearance of the Messiah, the King. But notice, they've been waiting a long time, implying that the story actually began much earlier, and is now concluding.

The parable centers around ten virgins, or bridesmaids, depending on which translation you prefer, awaiting the appearance of a bridegroom. The Greek word is **parthenos**, which always describes *someone who has never had sexual intercourse.* The use of the word bridesmaid comes from an attempt by translators to adhere to the context of the story. But in any case, here's where some knowledge of first-century Jewish wedding traditions comes in handy.

CAN I MARRY HER?

In those days, when a man took a fancy to a young woman, he approached her father to ask for her hand in marriage. A brief negotiation followed where they settled on the bride price: compensation for the family's loss of their daughter's productive value. If acceptable, and if the daughter agreed, they were officially betrothed, and he went away to build a home for them next to his father's house. This could take some time, and the couple rarely met again until the father of the groom pronounced the newly built home fit for habitation. Only then was the date set, and the man given permission by his father to go collect his bride for the wedding.

During this time, the young woman was to watch and wait. She and her bridesmaids were to maintain a constant state of preparedness since the wedding date would not be known to her until the bridegroom appeared. For his part, the groom would usually try to show up unexpectedly to surprise her, carrying her off suddenly "like a thief in the night" when no one would see them.

When the bridesmaids discovered the bride had been "snatched away" there would be a great torch-lit procession, announcing to the whole town that the wedding banquet was about to begin. This was typically a seven-day celebration during which the bride and groom were hidden away in their private rooms while the whole town made merry. The father of the groom picked up the tab for the festivities.

I CAN SEE CLEARLY NOW

Against the backdrop of this tradition, the meaning becomes clear when we insert the actual characters those in the parable represent. To do this, we'll rely on the principle of Expositional Constancy, from which we learn that symbolism in Scripture tends to be consistent. For example, whenever yeast is used symbolically it always refers to sin, while symbolic use of the word rock always refers to the Lord, etc. All through the Scriptures, whenever the term bridegroom is used symbolically, it always refers to the Lord. And no one argues that the Bride of Christ is uniquely descriptive of the Church. Obviously, the bridesmaids are not the Bride so they can't represent the Church. In fact, the Bride is never mentioned anywhere in the parable. She was obviously spirited away earlier while the bridesmaids slept. The bridesmaids represent people on Earth during the Great Tribulation after the Church has been spirited away in the Rapture.

GOT OIL?

Now it's time for the wedding banquet, but some bridesmaids lack sufficient oil to light the way. Asking to borrow some from their friends they're refused. There might not be enough to go around and so they set off to buy some for themselves. By the time they return, the banquet has already begun, the door is closed, and they're refused admission—the bridegroom claiming that he doesn't even know them.

Checking on the symbolic use of oil, we find it refers to the Holy Spirit. The Holy Spirit is a gift uniquely given to believers at the moment of salvation (**Ephesians 1:13**). You can't get it for others nor can they give any of theirs to you. Each of us has to receive it by ourselves and for ourselves.

The bridesmaids with oil represent those who will have given their hearts to the Lord during the Tribulation period after the Church has gone, while those without it symbolize others who haven't, and only those who have will be invited in.

WHAT'S THAT SUPPOSED TO MEAN?

So what does the parable mean? First, I'm convinced it's not trying to hint at the timing of the Rapture. I believe its sole purpose is to serve as one of the clearest warnings the Lord ever gave to those He would find still on Earth when He returns, and that's to make sure they're ready to receive Him while there's time.

When the Lord comes back at the End of the Age, He'll find both believers and unbelievers present on Earth. Having previously spirited His bride (the Church) away, He'll now decide who should be allowed to participate in the blessings of His Kingdom using the presence of the Holy Spirit in each one's life as the determining factor. Those with whom the Spirit resides when He returns are invited in but those without it will be excluded.

Because just as importantly, the parable teaches that His return signals the deadline after which even the request to be saved and receive the Holy Spirit will be denied. (The foolish virgins, as the story calls them, were on their way to get oil when the bridegroom arrived.) The door will be closed, and the Lord will deny ever knowing those who've asked too late.

By not deciding for Him, they will have decided against Him, and once His return proves them wrong, there'll be no opportunity to change their minds. For it is by grace that you have been saved, through faith (**Ephesians 2:8**) and faith is being sure of what we hope for, and certain of what we do not see (**Hebrews 11:1**).

Now you know the adult version.

CHAPTER FIFTY-FIVE

THE PARABLE OF THE TALENTS

IT'S NOT MONEY AND IT'S NOT SKILL. WHAT IS IT?

The Lord's use of parables always gets my interest. The Lord Jesus wasn't the first to use parables in His teaching, (there are many in the Old Testament, as you've seen in this book) but He sure elevated their importance in communicating Biblical truths to His listeners. His parables often angered the religious leaders of His day because they got the point of the story, and it was usually critical of them.

WHAT DOES THAT MEAN?

So we have three guidelines in interpreting parables: context, Scripture, and our old friend Expositional Constancy. Failure to follow them causes us to miss the point. For example, look at the way the Parable of the Talents has been interpreted, or should I say misinterpreted. One problem is that talent is also an English word meaning a skill or ability. But in the Greek language a talent was a unit of measure, and sometimes defined an amount of money. In dry measure, a talent was approximately 85 lbs. (34 kg.) and in money, equaled about 15 years income for the average person.

Since everything in a parable is symbolic, to think of the talents as being either a skill, as in the English or money as in the Greek is wrong, and distorts the message of the parable. Instead, think of the talent as symbolizing something of great value to the Lord, something that belonged to Him, that He entrusted to His servants while He was away, and that He expected them to invest for a return. (Since the Lord didn't leave a pile of money with anyone, you can see why money doesn't correctly define the symbolic talents.)

CONTEXT, CONTEXT

Now notice the time frame. The word **again** in **Matthew 25:15** identifies the time of the story as being the same as in the previous chapter, the Parable of the Ten Bridesmaids. That parable begins with the phrase "at that time" so you have to keep going back all the way to **Matthew 24:21 & 29** to discover what Jesus is teaching about occurs immediately after the Great Tribulation, when He comes back to establish His kingdom.

What will the situation on Earth be at that time? Follow the parable. He will have been gone for a long time and will have just come back. He will have left some valuable property of His in the care of His servants, and some will have multiplied it while others will have buried it. He now requires an accounting of them that will determine their destiny. The context tells us a lot, but what is His property?

IS THAT SCRIPTURAL?

This is where using Scripture to interpret Scripture comes in. We know from Scripture that money is not important to the Lord and that He is not limited to whatever skill we have and are willing to apply to accomplish His ends. But is there something of His, something extremely valuable to Him, prized even above His name, that He has entrusted to us, and that will be buried and all but lost to many at the end of the age?

SO WHAT'S THE ANSWER?

It's found in **Psalm 138:2** "I will worship toward thy holy temple, and praise thy name for thy lovingkindness and for thy truth: for thou hast magnified thy word above all thy name." (KJV) By adding a verse from **Amos 8:11** we discover that "The days are coming," declares the Sovereign Lord, "when I will send a famine through the land-- not a famine of food or a thirst for water, but a famine of hearing the words of the Lord." And in **Isaiah 55:10-12** we are told that His word, once invested, will always bring a return. It is His most valued possession, He left it with us, and He expects us to invest it (**Matthew 28:16-20**).

But the last days will be a time of deception so great that most of those alive on earth will succumb to a system of lies that will literally turn white into black, light into darkness, and therefore life into death. The only reference point for truth will be His Word, and many of those with whom it has been entrusted will have rendered it so meaningless as to be buried. The fact that those servants will have been imposters from the beginning is shown by their destiny: "outside, into the darkness, where there will be weeping and gnashing of teeth." (**Matthew 25:30**) The one and only unforgivable sin, after all, is unbelief.

Now you know the adult version.

CHAPTER FIFTY-SIX

THE LAST SUPPER

HE WHO WOULD BE FIRST MUST BE SERVANT TO ALL

It was the 13th day of the month the Jews call Nisan. It was getting close to sunset when, by tradition, Jewish families slaughter the Passover Lamb. So the disciples asked Jesus where He wanted to celebrate Passover.

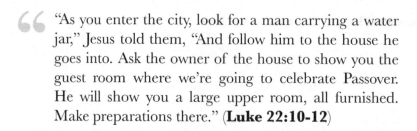

> "As you enter the city, look for a man carrying a water jar," Jesus told them, "And follow him to the house he goes into. Ask the owner of the house to show you the guest room where we're going to celebrate Passover. He will show you a large upper room, all furnished. Make preparations there." (**Luke 22:10-12**)

That wasn't as tricky as it might sound. All Jerusalem's residents were required to build an extra room on their house to give visiting pilgrims a place to celebrate the Holy Days. Also, men didn't carry water jars in those days (that was women's work), so the man was easy to spot. Everything else went as predicted and they had a room for the Passover.

WHAT DAY IS TODAY?

After the sun had set, it was officially Passover, the 14th. This was the day and time of the first Passover in Egypt, nearly 1,500 years earlier. Then the Israelites hurriedly ate a meal consisting only of lamb, bitter herbs, and unleavened bread. That afternoon, their doorposts had been covered with the blood of the lamb they had roasted and were now eating, and soon they would hear the cries of the Egyptians, who had not protected themselves from the destroying angel and would now suffer the loss of their firstborn.

During the time of Jesus, the 14th was known as Preparation Day. This day was spent getting ready for the festival meal, celebrated on the 15th, the first day of the week-long Feast of Unleavened Bread. Since the 15th was a special Sabbath, all the preparations had to be completed by sundown on the 14th. The ceremonial meal on the 14th was overshadowed by the great celebration the following day, but it was this meal Jesus and his disciples were now preparing for, and that explains how Jesus was able to both eat the Passover meal and die on Passover.

Remember, the Jewish Day begins at sunset and so the Last Supper, though eaten in the evening, was the first meal of the day. Following it, Jesus would be arrested and subjected to multiple interrogations and trials by the Sanhedrin, King Herod, and Pontius Pilate. He would be confined in a dungeon, flogged, crucified and buried—all within a 24-hour period. This was necessary to avoid having Him on the cross during the Sabbath, a violation of Jewish Law. (It's interesting that after all the laws they chose to break in executing Him, they obeyed that one.)

A MOVING EXPERIENCE

Jesus used this final time together to give His disciples one last preview of events that would soon transpire, comforting them as He did so, and promising them the Holy Spirit to guide them into all truth and help them remember what He had told them. He also changed their status from servant to friend. Friend was a more formal term in their culture than in ours and was used to describe a covenant relationship. By using it, He was bringing their association into the realm of the New Covenant. You could say the Church was born here. (These discussions are covered in depth in **John 13-17**.)

Just before the meal, He took water and a towel and washed their feet. This was a traditional preparation for the meal but should have been performed by a servant. The Lord was teaching them that He who would be first must be servant of all.

During the meal, the Lord instituted the memorial service we call the Lord's Supper or communion.

Distributing the unleavened bread, He said, "This is my body, given for you. Do this in remembrance of Me." He didn't say "broken" since not a single bone of the Passover Lamb could be broken in fulfillment of **Psalm 34:19-20**:

 A righteous man may have many troubles, but the LORD delivers him from them all; he protects all his bones, not one of them will be broken.

Then, taking the cup, He said, "This cup is the New Covenant in My blood which is poured out for many for the forgiveness of sins." As often as we eat the bread and drink the cup, we do so in remembrance of Him, till He comes. After the Second Coming, there won't be any more communion.

WHO STARTED IT?

The use of bread and wine in a covenant meal dates back to **Genesis 14:18-20** with Abraham and Melchizedek. And the two elements play a significant role in the circumstances that got Joseph out of an Egyptian prison to become Prime Minister of Egypt. There the bread symbolized death while the wine brought new life, just as it does in the Lord's Supper (**Genesis 40**).

Then Jesus said He would not drink of the fruit of the vine again until He did it again in the Kingdom. His last conscious act on the cross was to ask for a drink. As He drank the wine they offered Him, He said, "It is finished." The work was done, His assignment complete. The penalty for the sins of mankind had been paid in full. Phase one of the Kingdom had come.

After the meal, they sang a hymn. By tradition, this would have been **Psalm 118: 22-26**:

> The stone the builders rejected has become the capstone; the LORD has done this, and it is marvelous in our eyes. This is the day the LORD has made; let us rejoice and be glad in it.

This was the day appointed in history when the Lamb of God would die for the sins of the people and bridge that awful chasm between the Creator and His creation. This was the day when the bridegroom would pay the price for His bride. This was the day when Jesus, the author and perfecter of our faith, Who for the joy set before Him endured the cross, scorning its shame, and sat down at the right hand of the throne of God (**Hebrews 14:2**).

Let us rejoice and be glad in it.

Now you know the adult version.

CHAPTER FIFTY-SEVEN

THE CRUCIFIXION

HAS THE TRINITY CHANGED?

After 12 hours of abusive interrogations, multiple trials, and a flogging that nearly killed Him, the Lord had finally made it down the Via della Rosa, out the Damascus Gate, and up the hill to Golgotha, the skull. It was time to face His final ordeal, the most painful form of execution ever devised.

It's a slow and agonizing death by asphyxiation. Hanging by one's arms makes it impossible to breathe, and exerting any down force to relieve the pressure on the chest puts the body's full weight on the hideously wounded feet. After a while, the victim loses the will to endure the pain, and breathing gets harder and harder as the lungs fill up with carbon dioxide. Oh, for the luxury of taking just one deep pain-free breath.

For one like Jesus, who was already in deep shock from a flogging that had literally torn all the skin and muscle from His back, leaving His rib cage savagely exposed, the agony was unimaginable. But there was one even more severe punishment to endure, one that was uniquely designed for Him, one that no one before or after

Him could ever experience. And it's the only one that caused Him to cry.

"He was oppressed and afflicted, yet he did not open his mouth," Isaiah had written of this event, "He was led like a lamb to the slaughter, and as a sheep before her shearers is silent, so he did not open his mouth." (**Isaiah 53:7**) He had taken all they could dish out, without so much as a whimper, but now He cried out in a loud voice, **Eloi, Eloi, lama sabachthani?** —which means, *My God, my God, why have you forsaken me?* (**Matthew 27:46**)

WHAT IS THE MEANING OF THIS?

An incredible disclosure lies behind these few words. But first, it's a direct quote from **Psalm 22**, the most graphic description of what it feels like to be crucified anywhere in Scripture. It was written by King David 1,000 years earlier, before crucifixion had been invented, as a work of prophecy that Jesus and His executioners fulfilled in minute detail.

More importantly, this cry was the Lord's reaction to the ultimate penalty for sin—separation from God. The wages of sin is death, the Scriptures say, and the ultimate death is separation from God. To pay the full penalty due us for our sins, Jesus had to experience separation from God. That meant God had to turn His back on His Son, and when He did, light was taken from the world. From noon to 3:00 p.m. the day became as dark as night in fulfillment of **Amos 8:9**:

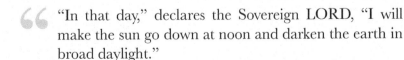

> "In that day," declares the Sovereign LORD, "I will make the sun go down at noon and darken the earth in broad daylight."

We don't know how that feels because our sin nature prevents us from having complete union with God. And we can't begin to describe it from a theological standpoint. But something awful happened that day, and the reason the Gospel writers left His cry in the original language was so we could discover it. The singular form of the word for God is **El**, and the plural is **Elohim**. Jesus used a dual form, **Eloi**, indicating that He was crying out to the other two members of the Trinity. Something happened to the makeup of the Trinity that day, and whatever it was, it was permanent. Jesus is still a man today. There's a man on the throne at the right hand of God.

> "Then I saw a Lamb, looking as if it had been slain, standing in the center of the throne," (**Revelation 5:6**).

That means that Jesus appears today just like He appeared to the disciples after the Resurrection, like a man. He has forever experienced some form of separation from God the Father and God the Holy Spirit.

Our Lord didn't just receive some "holy spanking" as some have described it, to pay for our sins. According to Paul He literally became the physical embodiment of sin, (**2 Corinthians 5:21**) so much so, that for the first time in all eternity, His Father could not bear the sight of Him.

> Your eyes are too pure to look on evil; you cannot tolerate wrong. (**Habakkuk 1:13**)

Our Lord loves us so much that to make it possible for us to have the full measure of our inheritance, He forever gave up a share of His.

Now you know the adult version.

CHAPTER FIFTY-EIGHT

THE RESURRECTION AND ASCENSION

AND YOUR JOY WILL BE COMPLETE

Jesus died around 3 p.m., long before sundown, on Thursday the 14th of Nisan—**Day one**. As the sun set, it became Friday the fifteenth—**Night one**. At sunrise, **Day two** began—still Friday. Remember, ever since **Genesis 1**, the evening has preceded the morning in Jewish timekeeping. At sundown Friday, it became Saturday—**Night two**. Sunrise brought **Day three**, still Saturday. And with sunset came Sunday—**Night three**.

Three days and three nights, or literally, three day seasons and three night seasons.

It was now just before sunrise on Sunday the 17th, and on the Jewish calendar, it was the first day of the week and the Feast of First Fruits. As the priests in the Temple prepared to dedicate the first fruits of the spring grain harvest to the Lord, Mary Magdalene, and the other women with her, hurried toward the tomb where Joseph of Arimathea had laid Him on Thursday. They hadn't been able to properly prepare His body for burial because of the special Sabbath on Friday and then came the regular Sabbath on Saturday. This was their first opportunity, and it was already three days since He had died.

As they hurried toward the tomb, there was a violent earthquake, likely caused by an angel of the Lord who had come down and rolled away the giant stone that had covered the entrance. When they got there the angel was sitting on the stone, dressed in white clothing so bright, it literally shone. The guards had passed out from fright, and the angel explained that Jesus wasn't there, He had risen from the dead just like He said He would.

YOU CAN'T BE SERIOUS

Mary ran back to tell the others, but of course, they didn't believe her. Finally, John and Peter went to the tomb and confirmed that it was empty, only the grave clothes remained there. After they had gone back to tell the other disciples, Mary wandered around, finally spotting a man she thought was the gardener. Asking where they had put the body, she was shocked to hear His voice speaking her name. It was the Lord!

As she clung to Him, He told her to tell the disciples He'd meet them all later since He hadn't gone to His Father yet. As our High Priest, it was His responsibility to sprinkle the blood of the sacrifice on the Mercy Seat in the Holy of Holies. Because the Temple on Earth was only a copy of the original in Heaven, He was going there to sprinkle His own blood on the Heavenly altar.

Later that day, two disciples walking along the Road to Emmaus were joined by a stranger. They later discovered Him to be the Lord. He explained to them all the Old Testament prophecies He had fulfilled in His death and Resurrection. Inviting Him to share a meal with them, they were astonished to see the scars in His wrists when He extended His arms to break the bread!

That night all the disciples except Thomas were in the Upper Room behind locked doors for fear of the Jews. Suddenly there was the smell of sweet perfume and the Lord stood among them. "**Shalom**

alechem," He said, "*Peace be with you.*" Breathing on them, He gave them the Holy Spirit He had promised four days earlier. The following Sunday night, the same thing happened again with Thomas there, who after seeing the Lord with His own eyes, finally believed.

 "You believe because you have seen," the Lord said. "Blessed are those who have not seen yet have believed." (**John 20:29**)

He was referring to us, who believe by faith.

Later Jesus appeared to the disciples on the shores of the Sea of Galilee, again calling them friends in recognition of their covenant relationship. There He restored Peter and placed him in charge, saying "Feed my sheep." (**John 21:15-19**)

He appeared to them frequently over the next 40 days, finally telling them to remain in Jerusalem until the Holy Spirit empowered them to begin their ministry to Judea, Samaria, and all the world.

Having told them that, He took them to the top of the Mount of Olives where He was taken up into the clouds and out of sight.

They were looking intently up into the sky as He was going, when suddenly two men dressed in white stood beside them. "Men of Galilee," they said, "why do you stand here looking into the sky? This same Jesus, who has been taken from you into Heaven, will come back in the same way you have seen him go into Heaven." (**Acts 1:10-11**)

Now you know the adult version.

ABOUT THE AUTHOR

Jack Kelley was a Bible teacher for over 30 years. He had a special gift of making the Word of God clear and easy to understand, and his teachings have impacted millions of lives. He simplified complex topics, and had an amazing ability to communicate the heart of God for His people. In addition to teaching, Jack served as a consultant, counselor, lay pastor, and missionary. All his teachings are available, free of charge, on his website gracethrufaith.com.

For more information
gracethrufaith.com
info@gracethrufaith.com

Made in United States
Orlando, FL
14 September 2023

36964310R00153